The Dance Book

555 Ways to Ask, Answer, & Plan For Dances

The Dance Book

555 Ways to Ask, Answer, & Plan For Dances

compiled by
Blair & Tristan Tolman

Coypright © 1997 Blair & Tristan Tolman
All Rights Reserved.

No part of this publication may be reproduced in any form or by any means without permission in writing from the publisher.

Printed in the United States of America

Contributors

Susan Adkins
Mike and Risa Ashment
Jan Babbel
Sasha and Brady Belliston
Meesa Bowen
Tonja Bowen
Daniel Brandt
Jenny Case
Justin Cash
Aaron Cordova
Brad Cowgill
Chris Cowgill
Linda Dastrup
Shirlee Dastrup
Chris Dummar
Kyle Dunn
Joshua Earnest
James and Mandy Facer
Trent Feist
Rebecca Gifford
Susie Greco
Erik Groves
Stephanie Haddock
Allison Hall
Jeff Harmer
Brad Hart
Betsy Hintze
Josh Hocker
Sarah Hocker
Jill Hormick
Todd Huffaker
Galen Hugger
Jessica Jacobson
Cory Jensen
Laura Jessop
Jared Jones
Jason Jones
Zeek and Shauna Kropf
Chris Klaich
Melissa Malott
Karl Martineau
Sonnet Martineau
Stan Martineau
Tamra Martineau
Justin McBride
Josh McCleery
Darrin McGowan
Rachele McIlroy
Stacey McIlroy
Karen Mease
Luke Mease
Christy Nelson
Jason Neuwirth
Alicia O'Brien
Dave and Teresa Oldham
AnJannette Olsen
Brad Olsen
Rob Owings
Janie Penfield
John Penfield
Casey Powell
Jacqui Rencher
Caterina Rossin
Aaron Seibert
John and Stephanie Smith
Nicole Smith
Amy Snover
Veldon and Diane Sorenson
Craig and Emlee Tanner
Jessica Tanner
Jim Thorderson
Sherrie Thornton
Mark and Becky Tolman
Steve and Lisa Tolman
Tirzah Tolman
Tricia Toponce
Adam Watkins
Greg Watts
Angela Waugh
Joe Weaver

Contents

Introduction 1

Chapter One:
Asking Someone To A Dance 4

Chapter Two:
Answering When The Answer Is "Yes" 45

Chapter Three:
Answering When The Answer Is "No" 76

Chapter Four:
Ideas For Dinner 85

Chapter Five:
After-The-Dance Activities 90

Chapter Six:
Planning A Dance 96

Chapter Seven:
Ideas For Dance Themes 102

Dedicated to the young people we teach, learn from, play with, and love. Thanks for keeping us young at heart!

Introduction

Part I

Jenni opened her bedroom door to an explosion of pink. Confetti blanketed her head and fluttered to the floor. The plastic pink cup, which balanced precariously on the upper edge of the door, toppled to the floor along with the shreds. Her entire room glowed pink, emanating from her two bedroom lamps which had been covered with pink plastic wrap. Pink helium balloons tied to curly pink ribbon floated up from her bedposts. Pink confetti covered the floor. Pink streamers hung from the ceiling and tickled her head as she walked across the room.

And, what was this? Her mattress was upside down, placing her bed sheets and blankets underneath the exposed underside of the quilted mattress. Her jewelry box was upside down, as were her senior pictures, all twenty three pair of her shoes in the closet, her alarm clock, and even the posters on her wall . . . it was all upside down!

Then, she found it, tied to one of the pink balloons—a card with her name written on it, in obvious male script. Her cheeks flushed and her heart fluttered with excitement as she tore open the card and read, "Jenni, I'd FLIP and be tickled PINK if you'd go to the dance with me! Love, Jaxon."

Part II

Jaxon, tired from his tennis match, waved goodbye to his doubles partner and approached his car. Fishing for his keys in his pocket, he noticed that something was stretched over the driver's seat of his car. Peering through the window, he recognized it as a T-shirt. Expecting an answer from Jenni, he fumbled excitedly with the car keys, opened the car door, and plunged his head inside. His heart sank as he viewed a big " No" written in solid black marker across the front of the shirt.

But wait, what was this? Below the "No" was a red "Yes," an orange "Maybe," and a green "I'll think about it." One sleeve read, "I have to wash my dog that night" and on the other sleeve was written, "This would be my dream date!" Confused, yet excited, Jaxon picked up the T-shirt for closer examination. The back of the shirt was filled with messages such as a purple "I just can't," a blue "I'd love to," and a yellow "Not on your life!" To make matters even more confusing, questions marks of all sizes and colors filled the empty spaces between the words.

What was he to make of this? He searched the car for additional clues, but to his frustration, found nothing. He drove home not knowing whether to bless or curse his buddy Carson, who had cunningly asked for his car keys after lunch, claiming to have left his homework in Jaxon's car.

By the time he pulled in his driveway, Jaxon had determined to call Jenni and get a straight answer, but as he walked toward the front door, he noticed a red construction paper question mark taped next to the doorbell. He opened the front door to reveal a trail of question marks which led him into the dining room, along the dining room wall, across the kitchen floor, downstairs into the laundry room, and right into the open basin of the washing machine where a small box of detergent lay. Catching on, he threw the T-shirt into the washing machine, dumped in the detergent, and ran a cycle. As the machine spun down and halted, Jaxon flung open the lid, grasped the twisted garment, and shook the wrinkles out. "Yes!" He shouted. All of the colored words and questions marks, which had been written on the shirt with washable markers, had washed away, leaving only the red "Yes" on the front of the shirt, which had been written with permanent marker.

Part III

Over the past few decades, teenagers and young adults in many areas have established a fun tradition in the world of high school and college dances—the tradition of asking and answering dates to dances in creative ways. Some of our best memories of high school and college are of the dances: planning dances, asking and answering our dates, and of course, dancing!

INTRODUCTION

This book will help you in nearly every stage of the dance event. It contains a chapter for dance committees to use in planning a dance, it contains a chapter full of potential dance themes, it contains hundreds of ideas for every budget to use in asking and answering someone to a dance, it contains suggestions for creative meals before the dance, and it contains a chapter on after the dance activities. It should be noted that some of the dinner and after the dance activities are taken from the author's previous book, *Dating For Under A Dollar: 301 Ideas,* and many more ideas for such activities can be found therein.

With a little creativity, many of the ideas for asking to a dance can be altered a little to be used in answering someone to a dance instead, and vice versa. It is our hope that this book will become a reference for you as you plan and prepare for dances of all kinds. Hopefully, these ideas will help you brainstorm and will spark your own creative ideas for use in the future. Have fun planning, and have fun at the dance!

Blair and Tristan Tolman

Chapter One

Asking Someone To A Dance

Alarm Clock

Get a small travel alarm clock. Set it to ring very early in the morning and hide it in his bedroom. Stick a note to the clock that says, "Not to ALARM you, but it's TIME for me to ask you to the upcoming dance. Hopefully, you won't be too TIRED to go with me!" He'll find the note after he's searched around his room for the buzzing alarm clock.

Aluminum Foil

With her parents' permission, decorate your potential date's room with aluminum foil. Lay it on top of her bed, wrap it around her things, and tape it onto her door. Stick a poster on her door that says, "Don't FOIL me now! ALUMIN-ate my life and go to the dance with me!"

Apples

Ask him to the dance with a basket full of green, yellow, and red apples. Leave him the following poem:

> To the dance that's coming up real soon, I'm asking you to go.
> I'd love it if you'd be my date and hope you won't say no.
> To answer me, please do this thing: return the proper color.
> Red is no, yellow is maybe, green is you'd have no other!

Archery

Purchase a child's archery set. Have it delivered to her with a note that has been pierced by the arrow. The note could include the following poem:

The archer who sent me is taking a chance
To see if you'll accompany him to the next dance!

I came soaring high, and he will too
If you'll say "Yes" and make his dream come true!

Baby Picture

Get a baby picture of him from his parents. Frame it and give it to him with a card that says, "Hey, BABE! You've been FRAMED for the dance! Will you go with me?"

Baby Pictures

Get five pictures of you at different ages, one of you as a newborn baby, three of you as you grew up, and a current picture of you. Tape your newborn baby picture to her locker and attach this note, "This BABE is asking you to the dance!" Make a simple scavenger hunt for her throughout her school for her to find the rest of the pictures, which you have hidden in order according to your age, youngest ones first. She'll find your current picture last, which will finally show her who is asking her to the dance.

Balloon Bouquet

Give him a bouquet of helium balloons. In each balloon, include a slip of paper with one word written on each balloon, so that when every balloon is popped, he can arrange the words into the following message, "Will you go to the dance with me?"

Balloon Colors

Blow up a bunch of black and white balloons. Deliver them to her with a poem that reads:

> Black and white, wrong or right,
> Go to the dance with me on (day of week) night.
> Black means no and white means yes,
> Return a balloon so I don't have to guess!

Balloon In The Sky

Get a small log (about the size that would go in a fireplace). Put a note on the log which asks him if he can "LOG" you in for the dance.

Tie three helium balloons to the log: one red, one white, and one blue. Include the following poem with the note, and then hide:

> Please answer me now, I'm watching you!
> So here's what you have got to do:
>
> Let the red one go if your answer is no,
> Let off the white one if you might,
> And release the blue if you'd love to!

Balloon Letters

Write a message in balloon letters on a piece of posterboard which asks him to the dance. Cut each letter out and number each letter on the back so that as the letters are found, they can be placed in order to spell your message. Insert each letter into a balloon before filling the balloons with helium. Leave the balloons in his bedroom. As he pops the balloons, he must find the letters and organize them into the message.

Balloon Name

Purchase enough helium balloons to write one letter of your name (include both first and last name) on each balloon with a permanent marker. Tie the balloons into a bouquet and leave them in her room. Also, leave her this poem:

> Somebody's asking you to the dance,
> Hoping you might say yes, by chance!
> This bunch of balloons will spell his name,
> So figure him out through this little game!

Balloon Rainbow

Buy several balloons in the colors of the rainbow (red, orange, yellow, green, blue, indigo, and violet). Blow them up and tie them to a thick wire bent into an arch to resemble a rainbow. Deliver the balloon rainbow to his doorstep with a note that says, "You're the TREASURE at the end of my RAINBOW . . .Will you go to the dance with me?"

Balloon Room

Fill his room waist-high with balloons that you have blown up. In one of the balloons, insert a little piece of paper with your name on it before

ASKING SOMEONE TO A DANCE

blowing it up, so that it is inside the balloon after you tie it closed. Hang a poster with this poem written on it:

> We'd have a BALL if you would go to the upcoming dance with me.
> I'd FLOAT on AIR if you'd say yes, so happy I would be!
>
> You need to find out just who I am by popping these balloons.
> My name's in one, don't BLOW this chance, just answer me real soon!

Balls

Obtain a bunch of lightweight plastic balls at a toy store. Make a small hole in each ball (about the size of the top of a pencil). On each of several small pieces of paper write one of the words to this phrase, "We'd have a BALL if you'd go to the dance with me!" Number each paper so they can be placed in order. Insert one of the pieces of paper into each ball. Deliver the balls to him in a bag.

Bananas

For a group date to the dance, give her a bunch of bananas with an attached card that says, "A BUNCH of us would go BANANAS if you'd join us for the dance . . . Does that sound ap-PEEL-ing?"

Banner

Make a banner several yards long out of butcher paper. On the banner, write your message to her in symbols, like this: Would (picture of wood) You (picture of an ewe) Go (picture of a stoplight with the green light on) To (number 2) The Dance (people dancing) With (picture of a witch, then put "–C") Me (picture of you)? Fasten each wide end of the banner to a post and stick it in her front yard.

Beauty And The Beast

Ask her on a date to your house to watch the movie *Beauty and The Beast* with you. Before the date, get a video recorder and video yourself saying, "This BEAST would like to take you, the BEAUTY, to the upcoming dance!" Cue it up, so that after the movie is over, you can quickly pop it in your VCR and play it for her.

Bicycle Parts

Leave an old bicycle or several bicycle parts on her doorstep. Attach a tag with a funny saying on it to each part. Ring the doorbell, then run.

Ideas might include: "WHEEL you go to the dance with me?" (on wheel) "It would be TUBE-ad if you couldn't go with me" (on tube). "Please don't put your foot down on this plan" (on pedal). "Don't BRAKE my heart" (on brakes). "I won't be oFENDERed if your parents want to meet me" (on fender). "Are you TIREd of stupid puns? Then just answer me!" (on tire) "Can you HANDLE going to the dance with me?" (on handlebars)

Book

Create your own simple book using paper and a three-ring binder. Title the book, "YOUR MIND." Leave all the pages inside blank except for one page with a message written on it that says, "I've been trying to read YOUR MIND . . . Would you like to go to the dance with me?" Deliver the book to him.

Bookmark

Write your request for her to go to the dance with you on a bookmark and slip the bookmark into her favorite book sometime when she isn't looking. A simple bookmark can be made by laminating a strip of heavy weight paper (about two inches wide, six inches long), punching a hole in the top center of the bookmark, and tying a ribbon through the hole.

"Bounce" Fabric Softener

Give him a box of "Bounce" fabric softener with a note in it that says, "Would you like to BOUNCE with me at the dance? I won't CLING all over you."

Bowling

Invite your potential dance date to go bowling with you. Ask the person who runs the scoreboard to type a message onto the electronic scoreboard sometime during the middle of the bowling match. The message asks her to go to the dance with you. It might say, "You BOWL me over! Will you go to the dance with me?"

Boy's Life Magazine

Give her a *Boy's Life* magazine with a flyer inserted into the middle of it that says, "Put some LIFE back into this BOY . . . Go to the dance with me!"

ASKING SOMEONE TO A DANCE

Bubbles

Send him a bottle of children's bubbles with a note attached that says, "Don't POP my BUBBLE! Please go with me to the dance! I'll FLOAT on AIR if you'll say yes!"

Bug Splat

Find a bug splat on the windshield of his car. Make a big arrow and tape it onto his windshield, pointing directly to the splat. On the arrow, write, "This takes a lot of GUTS, but I was wondering if you'd go to the dance with me!"

Bunny Rabbit

Have a friend dress up in a bunny rabbit costume (or just ears and a tail) and deliver a bag of carrots to him with this poem:

> Some-BUNNY wants to go to the dance with you!
> If you CARROT all, HOP to it and find out who!
> Dial: (your phone number)

Include your phone number so he has to call it to find out who is asking him.

Burrito

Invite your date to dinner with you to a Mexican restaurant. Before picking her up, wrap up a note asking her to the dance in cellophane and roll it into the shape of a toothpick. After ordering burritos, excuse yourself to go to the restroom. Find your waitress and have her slip the note into your date's burrito before bringing it to the table. She will find the surprise sometime during dinner.

Butcher Paper

Get about ten to twelve feet of butcher paper. Write a large message on one side of it which asks him to the dance. On the other side, write your name backwards so that it would be read normally if viewed from a mirror. Post the banner off to the side of a road where he is sure to drive by and see it. He will see the sign and then (hopefully) read your name through his rear view mirror as he passes by.

Butter

Give her a stick of butter. Write this message on the butter wrapper, "You'd BUTTER go to the dance with me . . . It won't be a MARGINAL experience!"

Cake Mix

Decorate a box of cake mix and send it to him with a note that says, "I was having MIXED feelings on who to ask to the dance: the cutest guy or the smartest guy. Then, I realized I could ask them both by asking you . . . You really do take the CAKE! Will you go to the dance with me?"

Cakes

Make a beautiful, frosted cake and a small, burnt cupcake. With frosting, write "Yes" on the burnt cupcake and "No" on the beautiful cake. Leave both of them on your potential date's doorstep with a note that tells her to return her answer.

Camouflage Clothing

Dress up in camouflage army fatigues. Hand-deliver a note written on army-green paper that says, "I CAN'T SEE YOU going to the dance with anyone else! Will you go with me?"

Candy Bar Card

Create a candy bar card for him by getting a large piece of poster board and writing statements on the board to ask him to the dance. Glue on the appropriate candy bar in place of its corresponding word. For example, you might write, "U-NO you're a BIG HUNK with an EXTRA great personality. You could rule the MILKY WAY! I'd go BONKERS if you went to the dance with me. We'd be a SENSATION!" For a variety of ideas, go to the candy bar section of a supermarket and create your own statements using the candy bars for sale there.

Canoe

Take the person you want to ask to the dance on a canoeing date. While you're canoeing in the middle of a lake, give her a turn with the oars. Have a note taped to one of the oars which reads, "CANOE go to the dance with me . . . OAR not?"

Car Decorations

Decorate his car with balloons, crepe paper, and other party decorations. Cover his windshield with a piece of butcher paper with a message on it that asks him to the dance.

Car Message

Leave the following message on her car, "We AUTO go to the dance together. OIL treat you right. . .It'll be a GAS! We may get TIRED, but not EXHAUSTED. WHEEL you go with me?"

Chalk Drawing

Sneak up to the person's front porch or sidewalk during the night. Lay down on the cement in a position which looks like you have been killed and have a friend do a chalk drawing around your body. Rope the area off with yellow tape which says, "Restricted area." Using the chalk, write a message on the cement which says, "I'm DYING to go to the dance with you!"

Chalk Message

Write your invitation to the dance in sidewalk chalk on the road in front of her house or on her driveway. You could write your name on the cement driveway underneath her car, so she doesn't know who is asking her until she pulls out of the driveway.

Check

Give him a voided check from your checking account. Write his name on the "Pay to the order of" line, the name of the dance on the "Amount" line, and your name on the signature line. Attach a note that reads, "CHECK it out! I'm asking you go to the dance with me! Don't a-VOID me . . . Say yes!"

Chick

Buy a baby chick and give it to her with a note that says, "I'd love to go to the dance with a CHICK like you! Will you go to the dance with me?"

Chips And Salsa

Buy a bag of your favorite tortilla chips and some hot salsa. Send them to her with a note which says, "Some people think I'm a DIP, and you're definitely the HOTTEST thing around, so what do you say we CRUNCH together at the dance?"

Choose The Right

Make a large poster that says, "Choose the Right!" in large letters. In small script at the bottom of the poster, write, "P.S. I'm 'Right'!" and deliver it to her.

Christmas

To ask her to a Christmas dance, send her on a treasure hunt through the mall. The last clue requires that she have her picture taken with Santa Claus at the mall. Santa asks her to the dance for you.

Cinderella

Ask her to watch either the movie *Cinderella* or *The Slipper and the Rose* with you. Before the date, buy a pair of high heel shoes from a thrift store that are her size and spray paint them silver. After watching the movie together, pull out one of the shoes and slip it on her foot. Say, "I would feel like Prince Charming if you would accompany me to the next ball."

Clothes Line

String a clothes line across his yard. With a clothespin, hang this note on the line, "This isn't just a LINE . . . Will you go to the dance with me?"

Coloring Book

Purchase a child's coloring book and create a story that goes along with the pictures in the coloring book. You and your potential date are both characters in the story. Ask him to the dance in the story, and write the words of the story underneath the pictures in the coloring book. Instruct him that to answer you "Yes," he must color and return one of the pages.

Comb And Brush

In a basket, arrange a variety of plastic combs and brushes. Include this message, "Will you COMB to the dance with me? Please don't BRUSH me off . . . It won't be a HAIRY experience!"

Combination Lock

Purchase a long-stem red rose and a new combination lock. Put the rose in her locker at school with a letter which asks her to the upcoming dance. Attach the combination lock to the outside of her locker. Tape a note on the front of her locker that gives her Clue 1, which is the first

ASKING SOMEONE TO A DANCE 13

number of the correct combination for the lock. Clue 1 sends her somewhere to locate Clue 2, which is the second number of the combination. Clue 2 sends somewhere to locate Clue 3, which is the last number she'll need to open her locker. When she does, she'll find the rose and the letter from you. (Note: Only try this idea either right before her lunch break or right before school is out, so she is not late to any of her classes.)

"Cracker Jacks"

Purchase a box of "Cracker Jacks" (caramel popcorn with a prize inside). Slice an unnoticeable slit in the bottom of one of the corners of the box. Write a message which invites her to the dance with you and slip it inside the box. Then, find an appropriate occasion to eat the "Cracker Jacks" together. If she doesn't notice your note before she finds the prize, tell her you've heard that sometimes there are two prizes in a box of "Cracker Jacks" these days, and encourage her to look for a second prize in the box. The second prize is, of course, your note!

Crossword Puzzle

Write a message asking him to the dance. Using the words from the message, create your own crossword puzzle on a piece of graph paper and give it to him. For example, the message, "Adam, will you please go to Wild West with me?—Sarah" could be turned into the following crossword puzzle clues:

Down:
1. A legal document of a person's desires concerning the disposal of his property after death. (Will)
3. The father of the human race. (Adam)
5. A word used in politely requesting something. (Please)
7. The opposite of "me". (You)
9. Non-domesticated. (Wild)
11. Opposite of East. (West)

Across:
2. On your mark, get set, __! (Go)
4. Pronunciation of the second number. (To)
6. A word meaning "together." (With)
8. The wife of Abraham in the Bible. (Sarah)
10. The opposite of "you." (Me)

To make the crossword puzzle larger, you could add other words with definitions just to throw him off. At the bottom of the crossword puzzle, instruct him to read the answers to clues 3,1,7,2,4, 9,11,6,10,8 in order to find the message.

"Crush" Carbonated Drink

Purchase a few cans of "Orange Crush" carbonated drink, and a few cans of "Grape Crush" carbonated drink. Deliver them to her in a basket with this message, "I've had a CRUSH on you for quite some time . . . It would be GRAPE if you'd go to the dance with me! ORANGE you excited?"

Cupid

Have a friend dress up as Cupid and give him a plastic bow and some arrows with suction cup tips to carry with him. To each arrow, tie a note which asks her to go to the dance with you. During lunch or a break when she will be at her locker, have your friend prance through the hallway and shoot the arrows at her and at her locker.

Daily Planner

You may need to recruit the help one of her friends or parents for this one. Contact someone who could obtain access to her daily planner. Have him turn to the calendar section and on the night of the upcoming dance, write "DANCE with (your name)." Later that day, call her on the phone and ask her to check her calendar for that night to see if she is available to go out with you.

Dandelion Bouquet

Make a bouquet of dandelions and attach a card that reads, "It'd be DANDY if you'd go to the dance with me . . . No LION!" Give her the bouquet.

Dark Room

Purchase a box of black garbage bags. Tape them on the windows of her car, completely covering them. Inside the car, leave this message, "My life will be DARK if you don't go to the dance with me!"

ASKING SOMEONE TO A DANCE

Dates And Raisins
Give him a basket of dates and raisins. Include a card that says, "I hope this doesn't sound DRY, but I'm RAISIN' the question . . . Will you be my DATE for the dance?"

Dead Rose
Give her a dead rose with an attached note that reads, "Hey BUD, I'm DYING to go to the dance with a FLOWER like you."

Dessert
Take him out to dinner. Arrange with the waitress before the date to have a little note wrapped in plastic inserted into the middle of his dessert. When she brings his dessert and he begins to eat it, he'll find the note which reads, "Please don't DESSERT me for the dance! Will you go with me?"

"Ding Dongs" And "Twinkies" Cakes
Fill a basket with Hostess brand "Ding Dongs" and "Twinkies" cream-filled cakes. Place the basket at his doorstep, ring the doorbell, and run. The basket should include this message, "DING DONG! I'm ringing your bell to see if you'll go to the dance with a TWINKIE like me!"

Dinosaur
Get either a stuffed dinosaur, some balloons with dinosaurs on them, or some other dinosaur paraphernalia. Put them in your date's room with the following poem:

> Far away and long ago,
> The dinosaurs hoped you wouldn't say no!
> They told me last night in my sleep,
> (Date of the dance) you must keep!
>
> Because you're supposed to be my date,
> My asking you is probably fate.
> The dinosaurs are gone, but we're here to stay,
> So please go with me to the dance . . .
> I'll even pay!

Dirt

Fill a five-quart plastic ice cream bucket with ground up Oreo cookies (dirt) and spread a bunch of Gummy Worms through it. Also, put a little card with your name on it in the "dirt". Attach this poem to the bucket and deliver it to him:

> This just might be a DIRTY trick,
> But to the dance I'm asking you real quick.
> Dig through the dirt to find my name,
> Or eat it too, it's part of the game!

Dog

Give her a stuffed dog with this note tied around its tail, "Don't DOG me for the dance, please go with me! Make sure you TAIL me your answer soon!"

Doughnuts

Buy a dozen fresh doughnuts. Also, obtain a dozen little paper toothpick flags. (These little flags may be purchased at a bakery or a craft store.) On each flag, write a quality that you admire in the girl you are asking to the dance. Stab the finished flags into the doughnuts, one flag per doughnut. Deliver the dozen doughnuts to her with a message that says, "Here are twelve good reasons why I want to ask you to the dance. Will you go to the dance with me?"

Earrings

If she has pierced ears, buy her a pair of green earrings and a pair of red earrings. Wrap both sets of earrings in gift wrap and include a note which asks her to the dance. In the note, request that she answer you using the earrings: if she wears the green pair to school the next day, her answer is "Yes," but if she wears the red pair, her answer is "No."

Easter Basket

Prepare a goody-filled Easter basket for him. Make sure you include a few plastic eggs and put your invitation in one of them, or put one word of your invitation in each egg. Write something like, "You would make my Easter EGG-stra special by going to the dance with me!"

ASKING SOMEONE TO A DANCE

Easter Bunny

Purchase a stuffed Easter Bunny and several plastic Easter eggs. Inside each plastic egg, insert a small card with one letter of your name written on it. Hide the Easter eggs in his room and place the Easter Bunny on his bed. The bunny holds this poem:

> SOME BUNNY wants to go to the dance with you.
> I'll bet you want to find out who!
> Look for the eggs hidden in your room.
> They'll spell my name, so do this soon!

Electric Greeting Card

Purchase a greeting card which has the ability to record an audio message on it. Following the instructions, record a message on the card which asks her to the dance. Send the card to her in the mail or deliver it to her in person.

Envelopes

Stuff several envelopes with blank pieces of paper. Stuff one envelope, however, with a message on a piece of paper that says, "You're the MALE I want! Will you ENVELOPE me in your arms at the dance?" Put all the envelopes in a box and mail the box to his house.

Fairy Tale

Write a fairy tale about your perfect date. At the end, write, "Will you make my dream come true and be my date for the dance?" Deliver the book to her.

Feet

On a large piece of posterboard, draw two huge feet. Cut them out and put them on his doorstep or in his room. Attach this note, "It would be no small FEET for me, if you would go to the dance with me!"

Fire

For this idea, first make sure his home has a safe location on or near his front porch where he can build a very small bonfire. On his doorstep, leave all of the materials needed for the bonfire such as kindling, small sticks, and a match. Include some water also, so he can put the fire out. Leave him a note that reads, "I'd be on FIRE with joy if you'd go to the dance with me! Light this fire to say yes, or leave it alone to say no." Set up a tape recorder with the song "Light My Fire" by The Doors cued up and ready to play. Ring the doorbell, play the tape recorder, and hide. Watch from a distance to get your answer.

Fish

Fill her bathtub with water and put three live goldfish in it. Hang a poster over her bathtub which says:

> If FISHES were wishes, you'd have three.
> Would one of them be to go to the dance with me?

Flowers

Make several paper flowers out of colored construction paper. Tape them on the walls of his room and write this message on one of the flowers, "I don't want to be a WALLFLOWER, so please go to the dance with me!"

Flyers

Make up a flyer which advertises information about the upcoming dance and which gives several reasons why she would probably want to go with you. Put the flyer on her car windshield in the school parking lot. Be sure to put blank pieces of paper on all the other cars in the area, so the real flyer doesn't look conspicuous. Before doing this idea, make sure that distributing flyers on car windshields is legal in your area.

Foreign Language

Ask her to the dance in a foreign language. If she takes a foreign language class at school, you could ask her in class. Or, take her on a date to a restaurant that serves foreign food and ask her in that language. For example, to ask, "Will you go to the dance with me?" in Spanish, ask, "Iras al baile conmigo?" If you don't know a foreign language, try Pig Latin, "Illwa ouya oga ota etha anceda ithwa ema?"

Ghost

Make a ghost out of an old pillowcase or sheet and hide it in his bedroom closet with a note pinned to it that says, "Is there a GHOST of a chance that you would go to the dance with me?"

Glass Of Water

Deliver a glass of water and a note to his doorstep. The note asks him to the dance and provides him with three choices: if his answer

ASKING SOMEONE TO A DANCE

is "Yes," he is to drink the water immediately. If his answer is "No" because he already has other arrangements, he is to toss the water into the bushes. If his answer is "No" because he doesn't want to go with you, he is to dump the water on his head. Include a post script message at the bottom of the note informing him that you are watching for his answer from a hidden location. Ring the doorbell and hide somewhere nearby where you can't be seen, but where you can see your potential date when he comes to the door.

"Goldfish" Crackers

Buy a big box of cheddar "Goldfish" crackers from your local supermarket. With the permission of your date's parents (if necessary), spread the goldfish around his bedroom, but try to keep them out of the carpet. Buy one real goldfish in a goldfish bowl. Put it in his room also with a note taped to the fish bowl that reads, "Out of all the FISH in the sea, you are the one for me. Will you go to the dance with me?"

"Gummy Fish" Candies

Wrap several "Gummy Fish" gummy candies in a small net with a note that says, "I've looked at all the FISH in the SCHOOL and decided that the best CATCH would be you. Will you go to the dance with me?"

Hand

Get a fake hand at a costume shop. Purchase a box of candy and put the fake hand in the box with the candy. Include a note that says, "Will you accept my HAND for the dance?" Deliver the box.

Hangers

Get a few dozen wire clothing hangers and hang them all over her front yard. Attach a note to one of them that says, "Will you HANG with me at the dance?"

Hangman

Ask one of her school teachers to play a quick round of Hangman during class. The phrase that the class will try to guess should ask him to the dance from you. It could say something like, "(Her name), will you HANG with this MAN (Your name) at the dance?"

Hat

Put a note inside a hat that says, "I just HAT to ask you...Will you go to the dance with me? I'm BRIMming with fun." Deliver the hat to him.

Haunted House

Take your potential dance date to a haunted house, where you have previously given one of the ghouls in the haunted house a rolled up scroll with a ribbon around it which contains a message asking her to the dance. As you go through the haunted house with her, the ghoul scares her and then gives her the scroll. The message may include this poem:

> Halloween is coming soon, the ghouls won't stay inside.
> They make us shiver, make us shriek, and make us run and hide.
>
> This ghoul, although quite scary, has a message just for you.
> (Your name) would like to take you to the upcoming dance real soon.
>
> So go with him, he'll keep you safe, he's not real scary or mean!
> If you do go, you're sure to have a happy Halloween!

"Head And Shoulders" Shampoo

Give him a bottle of "Head and Shoulders" brand shampoo. Tie a note to the bottle that says, "Would your HEAD AND SHOULDERS accompany the rest of you to the dance with me? Don't be FLAKY . . . Say yes!"

Helium Balloon

Give him a helium balloon with a note either attached to the string or put inside of the balloon. The note says, "I'm RISING to the occasion . . . Will you FLOAT to the dance with me?"

"Hershey Kisses" Basket

Empty a bag of "Hershey Kisses" chocolate candies into a basket. On a small piece of paper, write, "Will you go to the dance with me?" Remove one of the "Hershey Kiss" tags and replace it with your note. Hide that kiss among the rest of the kisses. Then, tie this note on the handle of the basket:

> There are many kisses here, you may think, how queer!
> But if you look close, and take a dose,
> You'll soon find out what this is all about.

Leave the basket on her doorstep, ring the doorbell, and run.

ASKING SOMEONE TO A DANCE

"Hershey Kisses" Bedroom

Spread a bunch of "Hershey Kisses" chocolate candies on the floor of your potential date's bedroom. Leave a note on his bed which says, "Now that I have KISSED the ground you walk on, will you go to the dance with me?"

Hieroglyphics

Create your own alphabet of simple hieroglyphics. For example, a picture of an apple could symbolize the letter "A," a bow and arrow could symbolize "B," a cat could symbolize "C," and so on. Then, on parchment paper or another type of paper that resembles papyrus, write a message in hieroglyphics which asks him to the dance. When you give it to him, be sure to include a copy of your alphabet so he can translate the message.

Home Hunt

Send your potential date on a treasure hunt throughout her home to ask her to the dance. A sample treasure hunt follows:

> A dance is coming up, you know, it's time to get a date.
> You're going on a treasure hunt that will surely be first rate!
>
> I have assembled an impressive treat to ask you to this dance.
> Your job is to figure out who I am. Hurry up, now's your chance!
>
> Your first clue is hidden by a game your family likes to play.
> It's entertainment for one and all, and amuses you each day!
>
> *(Clue #2 is by the Nintendo)*
> Good job! You have started off well but you've only just begun.
> Look where you pour in the "Cascade" and you'll have almost won!
>
> *(Clue #3 is in the dishwasher)*
> You did it again! You're really swell, this one is a piece of cake.
> Look where you put wet clothes, it dries them with a shake.
>
> *(Clue #4 is in the clothes dryer)*
> Ha, ha, ha, good one, eh? Your next one takes more thought.
> Look where you choose clothes to wear, a dresser it is not.
>
> *(Clue #5 is in her bedroom closet)*
> "You're not bad! You need more clues to really make you think.
> The next clue is where food is cooked and it's not the kitchen sink!

(Clue #6 is on the stove)
Wow! If your mom could see this, she'd really be impressed.
Now go to where a person bathes, you can do it, you're the best!

(Clue #7 is in the bathtub)
That was tough, you're doing fine, now concentrate on this:
Look beneath the place you sleep, and be careful, don't you miss!

(Clue #8 is under her bed)
That was hard, but keep it up. For the next clue, you have pride.
In it, you drive around, and there's a dent in its left side.

(Clue #9 is in her car)
Hallelujah! The next clue is last, you'll end this by tonight!
Your prize is where a fire is built to keep you warm at night.

(Prize is in the fireplace)
You won the game! Fantastic! Now this message is for you:
If you're not busy Friday night, I'd love to dance with you!

Homemade Commercial

Tape a homemade video commercial into the middle of a movie which you have chosen to watch with your potential dance date. Ask him to the dance in the commercial. An idea for a commercial: if the dance is a formal, your commercial might be an advertisement for evening gowns or tuxedos.

Homing Pigeon

Deliver a homing pigeon to your potential date in a cage with a note that asks him to the dance. Tell your date to attach his answer to the pigeon and return it home by releasing it. Make sure you know where the pigeon's home is before attempting this idea!

Hot Dogs

Write a note which says something like, "Don't be a WEENIE, go to the dance with me!" Roll it up in cellophane and give him a hot dog with this note burrowed into the bun of the hot dog.

Hunger Strike

Stage a hunger strike outside her house. Sit on her front lawn just before she arrives home and hold up a sign that says, "I'm on a HUNGER STRIKE

ASKING SOMEONE TO A DANCE 23

with the exception of (name of your favorite candy bars) until you agree to go to the dance with me!" Sit there and eat your favorite candy bars as she arrives home to find you there. For an extreme effect, with her parents' permission, mow the lawn with the exception of the small section where you plan to sit. Wear grubby clothing.

Hunter

Give him an orange fluorescent hunting vest and a note that says, "I'm HUNTING for a DEER to go to the dance with me! If your answer is yes, wear this vest tomorrow during the even periods; if it is no, wear this vest during the odd periods. I'll be SCOPING out your answer!"

Hunting Target

Give her a hunting target and a note that says, "Are you GAME to go to the dance with a DEER like me?"

Intercom

If your school administration will allow you to use the intercom system during morning announcements or some other time, ask her to the dance over the intercom system.

Iris

Give him an iris with the following message, "IRIS-k a lot in asking you, in case you say no, but will you go to the dance with me?"

Jars

Obtain a gallon-size jar, a quart-size jar, and a pint-size jar. (Canning jars or milk cartons in these three sizes work well for this idea.) Give her all three jars and this note, "I may not be a GALLON-t man . . . I'm actually just a little PINT . . . but I'd sure like to QUART you! Will you go to the dance with me?"

"Jello" Goldfish Bowl

Prepare a box of blue "Jello" in a clear bowl. After it has set, place either orange goldfish crackers or "Gummy Fish" gummy candies on the "Jello". Beneath the bowl, facing upwards so it can be read through the "Jello," tape a note which reads, "Out of all the FISH in this lake, you're the one I'd like to take! Will you go to the dance with me?" Leave it at his home for him.

Jungle Animal

Give him a stuffed jungle animal and attach a collar with a tag that says, "Come SAFARI with me at the dance! I won't MONKEY around, no LION!"

Leaves

Put a big pile of leaves on her front lawn and a poster in the middle of them that says, "Don't LEAF me alone for the dance! Please go with me!"

Licorice

Purchase several boxes of licorice twists. Arrange them attractively in a basket. Using licorice whips or ropes, tie bows onto the handle of the basket. Leave a note in the basket which says, "I'd love to TWIST with you at the dance . . . Are you inTWISTed in going with me?"

"Life Savers" Candies

Purchase several packages of "Life Savers" candies, open the packages, and take all of the "Life Savers" out. Tape them all over his car windows, and cut a big circular "Life Saver" out of a colored piece of posterboard. On the posterboard, write, "You would be a LIFE SAVER if you would go to the dance with me!"

Lips

Bake a cake and cut it into the shape of lips. Frost it red or pink and write on it with frosting, "Hey, HOT LIPS! Will you go to the dance with me?" Deliver the cake.

Lipstick Mirror

With his parents' permission, write with a tube of lipstick on his mirror, "Will you STICK with me at the dance?"

Lipstick Windows

Apply a heavy dose of bright lipstick to your lips and kiss his car windows in several places, leaving lip marks all over his car windows. (You'll probably want to wash the windows before pressing your lips to them.) With your tube of lipstick, write a note on his car windshield which says, "I'm KISSING up to you, will you go to the dance with me?"

ASKING SOMEONE TO A DANCE 25

Lobster
Purchase a live lobster from a grocery store and put it in a large bucket of water. Leave it on her doorstep with a note that says, "I'd love to CATCH you for the next dance!"

Love Song
Have your younger brothers and sisters ring his doorbell. When he answers, have them sing him a love song. At the end of the song, they present him with a card asking him to the dance.

Macaroni And Cheese
Cook up a pot of macaroni and cheese. Inside of it, place a note wrapped in tin foil or plastic wrap. The note says, "I'm off my NOODLE for you . . . Will you please say CHEESE with me at the next dance?" Deliver it to him hot.

Macaroni Noodles
Purchase a bag of elbow macaroni from the supermarket. Pour the macaroni into a clear jar. On a tiny piece of paper, write a message that asks him to the dance. Roll the paper up as small as possible and insert it into one of the dry macaroni noodles before adding it to the jar. Deliver the macaroni to her with a message that tells her to look inside the jar for a message.

Magazine Message
Search through several magazines to find good phrases to describe your date or the fun time you would have at the dance together. Advertisements with large print work well. Glue the phrases onto a piece of banner paper so that when read all together, they form an invitation to the dance. Hang the banner in his room.

Magnet
Give him a large magnet with a card that says, "I've been ATTRACTED to you for some time now . . . Will you go to the dance with me?"

Make Up
Buy her a child's set of pretend make up and wrap it up as a present. Include a message in the present that says something like, "I'm just your BASEic kind of guy, trying not to BLUSH by asking you this. Do EYE

have a SHADOW of a chance of going to the dance with you? I'm not asking for your LIPs to STICK to mine, just for you to dance with me!" Deliver the present to her.

Mangos

Buy some ripe mangos and arrange them attractively in a basket. Put a picture of the guy you want to take to the dance in the basket with the mangos. On the top of the basket, attach a wide arrow which points downward to his picture. On the arrow, write, "Can this MAN-GO to the dance with me?" Deliver the basket to his house.

Matches

Purchase a large box of wooden matches. Write one tiny letter on each of several of the matches that will spell out, "We'd make the HOTTEST MATCH at the dance! Will you go with me?" Number the matches so that she can put them in order to read the message. Stick these matches in with the rest of the matches in the box and deliver the box to her. Attach a note that says, "HOT message inside."

Math Book

Create a story problem and have someone in his math class slip it into his math book on the page of his homework assignment. The story problem should also have a reference on it that states that the answer is in the back section of his book, on a given page. On the selected page, have the person place a paper with something like this written on it:

> The most correct solution to this problem would be
> For you to go to the dance with me!

Math Class

If you and your potential date have math class together, pre-arrange with your math teacher to help you out with this idea. Have your math teacher give the class a mathematical story problem dealing with the expenses of the upcoming dance. Ask the teacher to use your name in the problem, 'just for an example.' After the equation is solved, the teacher says, "Well, class, now that he's got the money part of it straight, all he needs is a date. (Her name), will you go to the dance with him?"

Meatloaf

Deliver a homemade meatloaf to his house. Inside of it, place a laminated or plastic wrap-covered note which says, "I've never been one to LOAF around. Will you MEAT me for the dance?"

Media

With his parents' permission, make a huge banner to put on his front door which reads, "It's in the newspaper and on the TV!" Then, make several flyers which say, "Will you go to the dance with me?" Tape these flyers to the screen of each TV in his home and insert a flyer in his family's daily newspaper. If possible, arrange with his family beforehand to allow him to open the newspaper before anyone else.

Milk

Purchase a carton of 2% milk and a carton of whole milk. Give her both of them with this message, "Is there a TWO PERCENT chance you'd go to the dance with me? I want to spend the WHOLE event with you!"

Mirror

After obtaining access to the mirror in either her bedroom or bathroom, draw a picture or message on it using dry erase markers which asks her to the dance. A rose in a vase next to the mirror would add a nice touch.

Model Airplane

Purchase a model airplane kit, open it carefully, and place a note inside which says, "I may not be a MODEL, but I would PLANE love it if you would go to the dance with me!" Wrap the model airplane up as a present and deliver it to him.

Monkey

Buy him a stuffed monkey and a bunch of bananas. Put the bananas in the monkey's arms with a note that says, "I'm not MONKEYing around, I'd go BANANAS if you would HANG at the dance with me!" Deliver the monkey to him.

Music Lyrics

Type the lyrics of a popular song that your potential date likes. While you're typing them, hide a message in the lyrics by typing each letter of your message in bold type. Give the lyrics to her and let her read through them and figure out the big question.

Name Tags

Buy a piece of posterboard and a hundred or so name tags, the more the merrier. Write different guys' names on each of the name tags. Write your own name on one of the name tags and draw a star on the reverse side of the tag. On the posterboard in big, bold letters, write the name of the girl you are asking to the dance. Below her name, write, "TAG, you're it! I want to go to the dance with you! To find out who I am, search for the star." Then, stick the name tags all over her bedroom on any item from which they will safely peel off, name-side-up.

Newspaper Advertisement

Put an advertisement in the classified section of your newspaper that says, "WANTED: (Her name) to go to the dance with (Your name). If you are (Her name), please respond by calling (your phone number)." Leave her a note in her locker that tells her to look in the classified section of the newspaper on the day the ad will run.

Nuts

Give him a can of nuts with a message that says, "I'll go NUTS if you don't go to the dance with me!" Or write, "I'm NUTS about you . . . CAN you accompany me to the dance?"

Nuts And Bolts

Give your potential date a box full of screws, nuts, bolts, and nails. Include the following note inside the box, "Finding a good looking guy like you is HARD WARE I come from, and it drives me NUTS to beat around the bush. That's why I thought I'd just hit the NAIL right on the head and ask if BOLT of us can go to the dance together. It may sound SCREWy, but I think the TOOL of us would leave the others LAGging behind."

"Oreo" Cookies

Purchase a package of "Oreo" cookies. Carefully unwrap the package, trying to open it at the seams so that you can inconspicuously glue it back together. Write a message asking him to the dance on little, white, circular pieces of paper, about the size of the Oreo frosting circles, one

ASKING SOMEONE TO A DANCE

word on each circle. Randomly select "Oreos" from the package, pulling them apart to expose the white middles. Place one of the words of the message on each circle of frosting, and then reassemble the "Oreos" and place them back inside the cookie package. After sealing the package of cookies, deliver it to him with a note which says, "Fiddle with the middle till you figure out the riddle."

Overhead

Write a creative message which asks your potential date to the dance, and make an overhead transparency copy of the message with a copy machine. Give the transparency to one of her teachers and ask the teacher to display the overhead for a short time during class.

Painted Tummies

You will need the help of some other male friends to do this idea. Just before a school sports event, get your buddies together and have each of them use fingerpaint or some other type of washable paint to paint one word of a message which asks her to the dance for you on his chest. Paint, "Will" on the first guy's chest, "You" on the second guy's chest, "Go" on the third guy's chest, and so on until you have finished painting your message. Be sure you all allow the paint to dry before putting your shirts back on. During the game, sit together in order, so that your stomach words line up to form the message. When the girl you are asking to the dance walks by, call out her name. After she looks at you, stand up and lift your shirts to reveal the question.

Pancakes

Deliver a homemade breakfast including pancakes to him on a fancy tray one morning. Leave this note on the tray, "My spirits will be FLAT as a PANCAKE if you say no . . . Will you go to the dance with me?"

Pansies

Give him a bouquet of pansies with a card that says, "Please don't be a PANSY . . . Go to the dance with me!"

Peaches

Give him either a jar of canned peaches or a basket of fresh peaches. Tie this message to the top of the jar or basket, "It'd be PEACHY keen if you'd go to the dance with me . . . And it'd be the PITS if you said no!"

Peanuts

Buy a large bag of peanuts with the shells still on them. Separate the nuts so that you only use the ones that have two peanuts in each nutshell. Tie sections of a long piece of string or yarn around the middle of each peanut. Hang the string of peanuts all over his front porch with a poem like this one:

> I'm a NUT HANGING around as you can see,
> And I've no one to go to the dance with me!
>
> So if you're as crazy and free as I,
> Answering me should be easy as pie!
>
> Will you HANG with me at the upcoming dance?
> NUTS come in pairs, so here's your big chance
>
> To share a night full of fun and laughter
> With a girl who's a NUT before, during, and after.

Pears

Give her either a jar of bottled pears or a basket of fresh pears. Include a card that says, "We'd make a great PEAR at the dance! Will you go with me?"

Personal Clues

Each day for five days, leave a clue about yourself in your potential date's locker. On the first day with Clue #1, let her know that you are asking her to the dance. On the fifth day, with the last clue, reveal your name.

Photo Booth

Go to a photo booth where you can have a strip of four photos taken of yourself. In the first photo, hold up a sign that says, "Will you." In the second photo, hold up a sign that says, "Go to." In the third photo, hold up a sign that says, "The Dance." In the fourth photo, hold up a sign that says, "With Me?" Give him the strip of photos.

Photographs

Take the following five photographs of yourself: 1) one of your feet, 2) one of your feet and lower legs, 3) one of your feet, legs and waist, 4) one of your body from the neck down, and 5) one of your whole

ASKING SOMEONE TO A DANCE

body. On the first day, leave the photograph of your feet for your potential date with a note that says, "You're being asked to the dance by . . ." and the photograph of your feet. On the second day, leave the second photograph, on the third day, leave the third photograph, on the fourth day, leave the fourth photograph, and on the fifth day, leave the photograph of your whole body.

Pictures

Tape a picture of you and a picture of her side by side on a piece of paper and write, "Dance?" below the pictures. Tape the paper in her locker.

Piñata

Make a piñata and fill it with candy and a message that reads, "I'm BURSTING to go to the dance with you!" Give it to her. (Instructions for making a simple piñata: Blow up a balloon. Tear newspaper into long, thin strips and dip the strips into a runny paste of flour and water. Smooth the strips onto the balloon. Cover the entire balloon with two or three layers of pasty strips. Allow the piñata to dry for a few hours outside, or dry it yourself with a blow dryer. When the newspaper is dry, decorate the piñata with crepe paper and glue. Then pop the balloon inside by pushing a pin through the hardened piñata. Cut a two-inch hole at the top and fill the piñata with candy or other treats and your message.)

Pine Cones

Arrange a bunch of pine cones in a basket. Tie a note to the basket that says, "My heart's been PINING for a long time . . . CONE you go to the dance with me?"

Pirate

Dress up in a pirate costume complete with eye patch, bandanna, peg leg, and sword. Go to her door, ring the doorbell, and announce when she answers the door, "Ahoy, MATIE! I'd TREASURE a dance with ye, if yer willin' to go with a PEG LEG like me!"

Pizza And Pizza Box

Buy a pizza from your local pizzeria. Write on the box, "Will you go to the dance with me? If your answer is yes, eat the pizza and return the box. If the answer is no, eat the box and return the pizza!"

Pizza Poem

Make a homemade pepperoni pizza for her. Arrange the pepperoni pieces into a large question mark before you cook the pizza. Put the pizza in a box and deliver it with this poem attached:

> I hope you will ponder as you look at this CRUST,
> If you'd attend the dance with me, I'd be so thrilled I would bust!
>
> We could smile for the photos, I'd be sure to say, "CHEESE!"
> Would you kindly share this SLICE of your time with me, please?
>
> If you will say yes, you'll have this guarantee:
> We'll make this PIZZA-our lives a fond memory!

Police Officer Arrest

Arrange with a police officer friend to drive to your potential date's house, approach his front door, handcuff him, and take him to the squad car. In the police car are a dozen long-stem red roses and a note that says, "Now that I have ARRESTED your attention, will you go to the dance with me?"

Police Officer Ticket

If you have a friend who is a police officer, have him pull your potential date over while she's driving her car to school, pretend like he's going to give her a ticket, and then, instead of write her a ticket, give her a note inviting her to go to the dance with you.

Popcorn Bag

Give him a huge amount of popcorn in a bag with a note in it which says, "I'm POPPING the question . . . Will you go to the dance with me?"

Popcorn Door

With the permission of her parents, popcorn her door. Tape large garbage bags to the outside of the front door of her house, so they cover the entire entrance. Seal off the bottom of the garbage bags, but leave the top open. Pour a bunch of homemade popcorn (do not salt or butter it) down through the top opening to fill the gap between the garbage bags and the door. Also, drop in a note that says, "I'd FALL AT YOUR FEET if you'd go to the dance with me!" Ring the doorbell. When she opens the door, the popcorn will fall in.

Portfolio

Look through magazines and cut out pictures of several female models. Paste each one onto a piece of heavy paper and, as professionally as possible, create a fact sheet for each of them, listing their talents, hobbies, and interests. With a photograph of yourself, make a fact sheet for you as well, and make sure you add lots of good things about yourself so that you are the obviously most desirable choice. Arrange all the fact sheets together in a portfolio. Have a friend deliver the portfolio to him, telling him that he is in such high demand that she has been hired to book his dances for him. She should tell him that all of the included women have requested to accompany him to the next dance, and that he should read through it and select his date.

Present

Decorate a large refrigerator box from an appliance store to look like a huge present. Climb inside the box and have some of your friends deliver the present to her door, special delivery. For your sake, you may want to call first to make sure she's home. When she begins to open the box, jump out of the box and request your PRESENTS with her at the dance.

Pumpkin And Knife

Give him an uncarved pumpkin, a knife, and this poem:

> I'd love to take you to the dance. Will you go with me, by chance?
> To answer me, please carve a face into this pumpkin, it's no race.
> A smiley face means yes, you'll go, a frowny face means sorry, no.

Pumpkin Carving

Set up a time with your potential dance date to carve pumpkins together. Before you get together, cut a small hole in the bottom of her pumpkin and slip a laminated note up inside of the pumpkin which asks her to the dance. You might include this poem:

> Hey, PUMPKIN, you're my choice for the upcoming dance.
> I know if you'd go with me it would spark SEEDS of romance!
> Don't SQUASH my heart, please say yes! I'd love it if you'd go.
> You're the one for me, I FALL for you—ORANGE you glad to know?

Purse

Have a friend sneak a note into your potential date's purse which asks her to the dance. The note could say, "Your PURSE is a PURSE-nal place, so I hope you don't mind this PURSE-nal question in it: Will you share some of your PURSE-nal space with me at the dance?"

Puzzle

Put together a small puzzle. When you are finished, carefully slide a piece of posterboard beneath the puzzle and another piece on top. Sandwiching the puzzle between the posterboard, flip it upside down and slide it back onto the table. Write a message across the back of the puzzle which asks your potential date to the dance. Then, take the puzzle apart, put the pieces back into the box, and deliver it to him with a note that says, "PUZZLED? Flip over."

Puzzle And Balloons

Purchase a small puzzle, assemble it, flip it over, and write this message on the back of it, "I'm POPPING a PUZZLING question: Will you go to the dance with me?" Take the puzzle apart, insert the puzzle pieces into balloons, and then fill the balloons with helium. Deliver them to him.

Puzzle Heart

Cut out a large heart from a piece of posterboard. Write on the heart, "I can HEARTly wait to ask you this PUZZLING question . . . Will you go to the dance with me?" Cut the heart into little puzzle pieces and deliver the pieces to him.

Puzzle Hunt

Make or purchase a small puzzle that is made of only about 10 large pieces. On each puzzle piece, write one word of the message, "Will you go to the dance with me?" Place each puzzle piece in a different location where she will find them throughout the day, such as taped to the inside of her locker, on the windshield of her car, and on her front doorstep.

Radio

Call the disc jockey of one of the popular radio stations in your area. Ask him to ask your date to the dance for you over the radio. Then, either call your potential date and ask her to listen to the radio at that time, or

ASKING SOMEONE TO A DANCE 35

make plans to be with her at the time the announcement is aired, so you can listen to it together.

Remote Control Car

Attach the following poem to a remote control car:

> There's something I would like to know
> That has my heart RACING out of control:
> Is there a REMOTE chance
> That you'd accompany me to the next dance?

Put a note on her doorstep that requests her to come to the door. Ring the doorbell and then hide nearby. When your potential date arrives at the door, drive the remote control car up to her. After she removes the note, drive the car away. If you can, sneakily exit the scene.

Repelling

Take your future dance date repelling. On your way down the rope, place a note on the rock, so that she will read it on her way down. The note might say, "Will you HANG out with me at the dance?"

"Ring Pop" Candy Ring

Purchase a "Ring Pop" candy ring from a candy store. Give it to your potential date with a note that says, "I'm POPPING the question, will you go to the dance with me?"

Rocking Chair

Make a stuffed dummy and set it in a rocking chair. In the hands of the dummy, place a sign which says, "WOOD you CHAIR to ROCK with me at the dance?" Place the rocking chair and dummy on her doorstep. Ring the doorbell, give the rocking chair a push to start it rocking, and run. Be sure to get the chair back later.

Rocks

Paint the word "Yes" on a small rock that would fit in your pocket. Paint the word "No" on a very large rock that would take both you and a friend to lift. Leave both rocks on her doorstep, with a note that asks her to the dance and says, "Please return your answer!" Ring the doorbell and run.

Roll

With frosting, decorate a smiley face on top of a roll. Deliver the roll to him with this note, "I'M ON A ROLL, so I think you might say yes . . . Will you go to the dance with me?"

Rope

With her parents' permission, hide on the roof of your potential date's house right over the front door. Have a friend ring the doorbell and run. Arrange with her parents to make sure she answers the door. As she looks outside to see who rang the doorbell, lower a rope in front of her with a note on the end of it which says, "Just DROPPING you a line to say I hope you'll be mine for the dance!"

Royal Prince

For this idea, you will need the cooperation of a friend and a horse. Have your friend dress up as a joker. You dress up as a handsome prince and ride the horse. Carry some roses to give to your potential date. Make a scroll out of parchment paper on rolling pins for the joker to carry. Ride up to her house with the joker walking beside you. The joker rings the doorbell. When she comes to the door, the joker rolls out red carpet. You dismount and walk on the red carpet towards your potential date. Kneel down and bow before her, handing her the roses. The joker reads from the scroll, "You are officially requested to accompany this handsome prince to the dance."

Sandwich

Give him a sandwich with a laminated note tucked inside it. The note says, "I won't LOAF around in asking, will you MEAT me for the dance? We'd really HAM it up, and that's no BOLOGNA!"

Scarecrow

Make a scarecrow out of straw and some old clothing. Put it either in his family's garden or in his yard and attach a note to it that says, "I'm too SCARED to go to the dance alone. Will you go with me?"

School Report

If you have a school report due in the near future, type it up and ask her to read the rough draft and critique it for you. In the middle of the text, type a message which asks her to the dance.

ASKING SOMEONE TO A DANCE

Scrapbook

If you have been dating the same person for a long time and want to ask him to the dance, prepare a scrapbook for him that contains pictures and memoirs of things you've done together and places you've been together. On the last page, write a message that says, "Will you make another great memory with me? (Name of dance)." Leave the scrapbook at his home for him to find.

Sea Shell

Write this message on a piece of paper, and insert it into a large sea shell, "I hope I haven't MIST the chance, and I hope you aren't all TIDE up. CONCH you go to the dance with me? Please SEA if you can go!" Give him the sea shell.

Serenade

Serenade her at her bedroom window with a song you've written which asks her to the dance. Sing it either by yourself or with a group of singers.

***Seventeen* Magazine**

Give her a copy of *Seventeen* magazine. Inside the magazine, insert a flyer that reads, "I have SEVENTEEN reasons why I would like to go to the dance with you: 1) I like you 2) I like you 3) I like you" seventeen times. Or, you could write seventeen different characteristics about her that you like.

Sheep

Make a large cardboard sheep and stick it in her front lawn. Attach a message to the sheep that says, "I feel SHEEPISH asking you to the dance because guys FLOCK around you, but will EWE please go to the dance with me? I want to go with you BAAAAD."

Shoe Search

Leave one of your shoes on his front doorstep with this poem:

> The owner of this little shoe
> Would like to go to the dance with you!
> To discover who is asking you,
> Tomorrow, she'll wear the match to this shoe!

Make sure you wear the match to the shoe to school the next day with an un-matching shoe on the other foot. He'll have to carry your shoe around with him to figure out who is asking him to the dance.

Shower Message

With his parents' permission, write this poem on a tile wall of his shower with a dry-erase marker, after testing the marker on a very small area first, to make sure that it washes completely off with water:

> You're probably very dirty as you enter here this day,
> And you'll probably be shocked as you read what I have to say!
>
> You're a very busy person, so I thought I'd catch you here
> To ask an urgent question, that I want to make quite clear!
>
> I'd love it if you'd go with me to the dance on Friday night!
> But after you get really clean and don't look like a fright,
>
> I hope that you will answer me and maybe you'll say yes!
> You'd have a fun, terrific time, with (name), if you couldn't guess!

Singing Telegram

Write a singing telegram which asks your potential date to go to the dance with you. Enlist a friend who has a good voice to dress up in a costume and sing the song to her.

Skeleton

Make a paper skeleton out of white paper plates. Cut shapes for the head and bones and fasten them with paper fasteners into the shape of a skeleton. Stick the skeleton to your potential date's front door with a note that says, "I've no-BODY to go with to the dance . . . Will you go with me?" Or put, "It took all the GUTS I had to ask you . . . Will you go to the dance with me?"

"Snickers" Candy Bars

Buy one miniature "Snickers" candy bar, one normal size "Snickers" candy bar, and one king-size "Snickers" candy bar. Glue these candy bars onto a piece of posterboard in the appropriate places, creating a message which says, "How many laughs do you like to have on a date? If

ASKING SOMEONE TO A DANCE 39

you like just little 'Snickers,' then go to the dance with just anybody. If you like just normal 'Snickers,' then go to the dance with just anyone normal. But, if you like king-sized 'Snickers,' then go to the dance with me!"

Soda Pop Bottle

Purchase a bottle of her favorite type of soda pop. Using a candle, melt some wax onto the top of the bottle. Then, while the wax is still hot, quickly stick the candle on top of it, thus securing it to the bottle. Tie a pretty ribbon around the bottle and attach a note which says, "I'd be SODA-LIGHTED to go to the dance with you." Light the candle, deliver to her doorstep, ring the doorbell, and hide. (Don't leave the area until someone safely retrieves the burning candle.)

Soda Pop Cans

Stop by her house when you know she won't be home and leave her a six-pack of soda pop which has a note on it that says, "I POPped by, but you weren't here. I SODA want to go the next dance and was wondering, do you SODA want to go with me?"

Spice Basket

Purchase small canisters of the following spices: sage, oregano, dill, cayenne pepper, allspice, thyme, and parsley. Place the canisters in a basket with a note which says, "I may not be a SAGE, but I know a good DILL when I see one. It's about THYME I asked you to the dance. CAYENNE you go with me? ALLSPICE up your life a little if you will go, I might even dance to Elvis PARSLEY! Please let me know, OREGANO go with me?"

Spots

"Spot" your potential date's room by cutting out several hundred little circles out of many different colors of construction paper and taping them all over his room. On a big circle on his bed, write, "I hate to put you on the SPOT, but I was wondering if you'd go to the dance with me!"

"Starbursts" Candies

Arrange a basket or bag with a bunch of "Starbursts" wrapped candies inside. Tie a note to the basket that says, "I'm BURSTING to go to the dance with you."

Stop Sign

Make a large paper stop sign that says, "STOP and see how lucky I'd be if you would go to the dance with me!" Tape the sign to his bedroom door or locker.

Storybook

Purchase a storybook and change part of it by inserting an invitation to the dance into the plot of the book. You could then either read the storybook with her or give it to her to let her read it on her own.

Suckers

Arrange a basket full of suckers with a note that reads, "Don't be a SUCKER . . . Go to the dance with me!"

Superman

Have a friend dress up like Superman and go to his door with a cake decorated with the Superman insignia on it. Underneath the cake is a note which says, "Hey, SUPERMAN, would you go to the dance with me?" As he eats the cake, he will find the note underneath it.

Supermarket

While out with your potential dance date, tell him that you need to stop by the supermarket before going home. As you walk in the store with him, wink at one of the store employees who has been waiting for you to arrive. After a few minutes of looking for groceries, a voice comes over the intercom system, calls your date by name, and requests him to go to the dance with you.

Survey

Create your own survey. It could be made to gather information on just about any topic: school lunches, sports, or dating, for example. Insert a question in the survey that asks him to the dance, and give the survey to him.

"Sweet Tarts" Candies

Fill a basket with "Sweet Tarts" hard candies. Tie this note to the basket, "Hey, SWEETIE! It's-TART-ing to be time to prepare for the dance . . . CAND-Y go with me?"

Swing

Write the following message on a piece of paper, "Will you SWING with me at the dance?" Tape the message securely to the bottom of the seat of one of the swings at your favorite park. Later that day, take your potential dance date to that same park and swing with her for a while. While swinging, casually mention to her that something is stuck on the bottom of her swing. Encourage her to see what it is.

Tape Recorder

On a cassette tape, record phrases from different songs which, when listened to in order, tell a story that asks him to the dance. Either give him the tape, play it to him over the phone, or leave it on his answering machine.

Teddy Bear

Give him a stuffed bear and a note which says, "It would be un-BEAR-able if you didn't go to the dance with me!" or "I would be BEARY happy if you would go to the dance with me!"

Telephone Book

Obtain a telephone book and search through it to locate your first and last names. (Although you may not be listed in the telephone book, you will probably find two separate people with either your first or your last name.) Highlight your first name and your last name with a yellow magic marker. Leave a note on her car which asks her to the dance, but doesn't say who it's from. Leave another note in her mailbox, one on her porch, and another on her bedroom door. Finally, leave the telephone book on her bed with a note which tells her that the mysterious note writer's name is highlighted inside the telephone book with a yellow marker. She must look through it to determine your identity.

Television

Put an announcement on your local Community Upcoming Events station on television that asks him to the dance. Tell him to watch the station on the day that the announcement will run.

Thanksgiving

Fill a horn of plenty with some of his favorite things such as a cassette tape or compact disc of his favorite group, a candy bar or other treat, cologne, or even poetry if you know he likes a particular author. Attach a note to the horn of plenty that says, "You'd make me want to TOOT my HORN and you'd give me PLENTY to be THANKFUL for if you'd accept a date to the dance with me!" Deliver it to him or leave it in his bedroom.

Toilet Seat

Tape your potential dance date's toilet seat shut. Leave a note on it that says, "If you have to GO, will you GO with me?" Or write, "I'm not willing TOI-LET you GO, unless you GO to the dance with me!"

Town Treasure Hunt

Send him on a treasure hunt throughout his town to ask him to the dance. He will have to follow each clue to reach the end of the hunt to figure out who is asking him.

Tulips

Give him a few tulips and the following note, "I'd love it if your TULIPS would go with mine to the dance!"

Tuna Fish

Give him a can of "Chicken of the Sea" brand tuna fish with a bow tied around it and the following message attached to the bow, "Just CHICK-EN to SEA if you'd go to the dance with me!"

Uncle Sam

Buy a poster of Uncle Sam or dress up in an Uncle Sam costume, if you can locate one. Either carry the poster or wear the costume to her front door and ring her doorbell. When she answers the door, imitate Uncle Sam by pointing your finger at her and saying, "I WANT YOU to go to the dance with me!"

Upside Down And Pink Balloons

With her parents' permission, sneak into your potential date's bedroom while she is not home and tip as many small, unbreakable things upside down as possible. Tie pink helium balloons to her doorknob or somewhere else in the room. Leave a big pink sign which says, "I'd FLIP and be tickled PINK if you would go to the dance with me."

Vegetables

Give him a basket of assorted vegetables and this message, "Hope this doesn't sound CORNY, but will you PEAS go to the dance with me? If you CARROT all, you'll say yes, unless you've already BEAN asked!"

ASKING SOMEONE TO A DANCE

Vitamins

Arrange a basket filled with little bottles of various kinds of vitamins. Include this message, "Can't you 'C,' I want you to 'B' my date for the dance. Please 'D' cide 'B-4' it's too late!" We'll have one HEALTH of a time!"

Wanted Poster

Create a "Wanted" poster with his face on it and a message that says, "You are WANTED to go to the dance with me!" Hang the poster somewhere where he will see it.

Warm Fuzzy and Cold Prickly

Make a Warm Fuzzy and a Cold Prickly. A Warm Fuzzy can be made by gluing eyes and feet on a yarn pom pom. A Cold Prickly can be made by gluing eyes on a pine cone. Give both of them to him with this poem:

> Will you go to the dance with me?
> Return the one you want to be.
> (Warm Fuzzy = yes, Cold Prickly = no.)

Watermelon

Deliver a watermelon and a small jar to him with a big red ribbon around the watermelon and another around the jar. Include a note with his name on it and a message asking him to the dance. In the message, instruct him to eat the entire watermelon. If he desires to say yes, he is to return 5 seeds in the jar. If he desires to say no, he is to return 100 seeds in the jar.

Wire Whisk

Deliver him a basket with a bunch of fresh eggs and a wire whisk in it. Attach a note to the handle which says, "WIRE you WHISKing my heart away? Maybe its because I've been trying to BEAT a way into your heart for a long time. Will you go to the dance with me? I'd feel EGGstatic, EGGcited, and EGGstra special if you'd say yes!"

Wishbone

Give him a wishbone on a fancy platter. Include this card, "Know what I WISH? That you would go to the dance with me!"

Wonder Bread

Give her a loaf of "Wonder" brand bread with a note that says, "I WONDER if you would go to the dance with me and let me spend some BREAD on you."

Wood

Put a pile of wood on her doorstep. Set up a poster near the wood that reads, "WOOD you go to the dance with me?"

Yarn

String yarn in a maze through her yard, with the beginning of the yarn tied to something solid near her front door (like a railing) and the rest of the yarn woven all over her yard (like under and over a car, around a tree, and through a basketball hoop). At the end of the trail of yarn, leave a basket with some goodies in it and a note which asks her to the dance. Ring her doorbell and run, leaving behind instructions for her to follow the yarn to a treasure.

Yearbook

Give him a yearbook with a picture of you in it. Highlight your name below the picture and insert a note on the inside cover which says, "I was wondering if this YEAR I could BOOK you for the dance! P.S.: To discover who is asking you, scan through this yearbook and look for the highlighted name below my picture."

Chapter Two

Answering When The Answer Is "Yes"

Admit

Get your potential date's school principal to help you with this idea. Send a hall admit from the attendance office of your potential date's school to her while she is in class, informing her that she must meet with the principal immediately. When she arrives, the principal makes her nervous by asking her some questions, but finally delivers to her a bouquet of flowers and a message from you that says, "Yes!"

Air Freshener

Give her a can of air freshener with a note on it which says, "I CAN SCENT."

"Alka Seltzer" Medicine

Give him a box of "Alka Seltzer" stomach medication with a plastic cup in a small basket, and attach this message, "PLOP, PLOP, FIZZ, FIZZ, OH, WHAT A RELIEF IT IS that you asked me to the dance! Yes!"

"Alpha Bits" Cereal

Purchase a box of "Alpha Bits" brand cold cereal, open it, and remove all of the letter Ys and letter Ns and paint them black. Count them to make sure there is at least one more Y than N, and mix them back into the box. Seal the box of cereal back up and deliver it to him with a card instructing him to search through the cereal for the Ys and Ns and to count them. Tell him if there are more Ys, your answer is yes, but if there are more Ns, your answer is no.

Arrows

Give him some arrows that have pierced through a message with a target drawn on it. The message reads, "I AIM to go to the dance with you, Yes!"

Atlas

Give him a world atlas and a card that includes any/all of the following sayings, "Yes! ATLASt you have asked me to the dance! You mean the WORLD to me! Without you, the EARTH would stop SPINNING! OCEANS couldn't keep us apart! Now that you have me, you've got the whole WORLD in your hands!"

Baby Booties and Poker Dice

Deliver him a small basket filled with a few poker cards, a pair of dice, and some little baby booties. Include a card which says, "You took a GAMBLE asking me to the dance. Will I go with you? You bet your BOOTIES!"

Baby Things

Gather several baby items together like a diaper, a bottle, formula, a bib, baby food, a baby spoon, and a rattle. Arrange them in a basket and include this card, "Hey, BABY! I'd love to COO to the dance with you!"

Banana

Using a knife, carve your answer into an unpeeled banana. Taking the knife in your hand as if it were a pencil, scratch the word, "Yes" into the banana peel. Press just hard enough to break the surface of the peel. This allows some of the juices to come to the surface of the peel without cutting the whole banana open. The sections you have carved will turn brown in just a few minutes, and the message will be clearly displayed in brown against the yellow background of the banana. If possible, you should carve the message just a minute or two before delivering it. You may want to include a note with the banana which indicates that she should watch the banana for your answer to appear.

Banana Pudding

Give her a big bowl of banana pudding with an odd number of cut up, fresh banana slices mixed into the pudding. Attach this message,

ANSWERING WHEN THE ANSWER IS "YES"   47

"I'm not PUDDING you on . . . Your answer is in here! If there is an odd number of banana slices, the answer is yes, but if there's an even number of banana slices, the answer is no. Hope counting ap-PEELs to you!"

Beans

Buy a small bag of beans. Cut the top of the bag open, sneak over to her house, and lay the bag of beans on her doorstep on its side with about one third of the beans spilling out onto her front porch. Tuck a message inside the beans which says, "I'm SPILLING THE BEANS . . . My answer is yes!" Ring her doorbell and run.

Berries

Arrange a basket full of fresh berries, or make him a berry pie. Deliver it to him with this message, "I'd be BERRY happy to go to the dance with you!"

Bible Verse (Genesis)

Write the Biblical scripture reference Genesis 24:58 in lipstick on his mirror. The scripture states, "Wilt thou go with this man? And she said, I will go." Let him find the reference and look up the scripture when he gets home.

Bible Verse (Psalms)

Leave a sign on his bedroom door that says, "Psalms 40:8, First Line." The first line of this scriptural verse says, "I delight to do thy will."

Blue

Decorate his room with blue balloons, blue crepe paper, blue confetti, and blue cellophane draped over his lights. Place a blue piece of paper on his bed with these words on it, "It probably makes you feel BLUE to receive the answer 'No.' P.S. See closet." Tie several bright, colorful balloons in his closet. Include a bright colored piece of paper with these words written on it, "BRIGHTEN UP! I would love to go to the dance with you!"

Bonding Glue

Give her a tube of bonding glue. Attach this message, "I'm no JAMES BOND, but I'm STUCK on you! I'd love to go to the dance with you!"

Bookshelf

Arrange with his parents to hide your answer among several books in a bookshelf at his home while he is gone. First, write your answer using several words such as, "The answer to your question about asking me to the dance is yes!" Write one word on each of several small pieces of paper. Hide each piece of paper in a different book on the bookshelf, noting the book title, author, and page number where the paper is hidden. In addition to each piece of paper, leave him a clue to help him find the next piece of paper. Tape Clue #1 to the front of the bookshelf where he will be sure to see it. He will have to follow your clues and search through several books on the shelf to obtain his answer.

Bottle

Put a message in a bottle that answers him to the dance. Cork the bottle and leave it floating in his bathtub, swimming pool, or sink for him to find.

Bowling Pins

Purchase a plastic set of bowling pins, and set them up on his bed. Leave this note next to the plastic bowling ball, "You BOWL me over! Yes, I'd love to go to the dance with you!"

Bows

Tie bows of all different sizes and colors around objects either in her bedroom or in the interior of her car. Tie one outrageously large, beautiful bow in an obvious spot where she will readily see it, and attach a note to this bow which says, "All the other BOWS are nice, but I'm your main BEAU . . . Yes!"

Boxes

Get a bunch of used cardboard boxes from a grocery store. Fill her bedroom with them, putting a few of her unbreakable items in some of the boxes. Inside one of the boxes, leave her a message that says, "PACK your things, because we'll be MOVING at the dance . . . Yes!"

Breakfast

With his parents' permission, deliver him breakfast one morning. Give him his favorite kind of cereal in a clear bowl. On the outside bot-

ANSWERING WHEN THE ANSWER IS "YES"   49

tom of the bowl of cereal, secure a piece of paper that says, "Yes!" Make sure you tape it on with the word facing up into the bowl. When he finishes his cereal, he'll discover his answer.

Briefs
Purchase a pair of the largest possible size men's briefs. Write on them, "Let me be BRIEF: Yes!" Hang them in his room.

Bunny In A Basket
Give her a live or stuffed bunny rabbit in a basket. Tie this note to the basket, "I was HOPPING you would ask me! EARS my answer: Yes!"

Cake
Bake a two-layered cake. Write "Yes" on a piece of cardboard and insert it in between the two layers. He will find your answer when he cuts the cake.

Cake Capsule
Write "Yes" on a tiny piece of paper and insert it into a small gelatin capsule. Bake the capsule right into the cake. When you deliver the cake, make sure you leave a note with the cake that says, "Caution: Answer inside!"

Can
Put a can of something on his doorstep with a note on it that says, "I CAN!"

Candle
Tie this note to a candle, "No one holds a CANDLE to you. Yes!" Deliver it to him.

Candles
For this idea, call her parents in advance to ensure that she is home, that the driveway is clear, and that outside lights are off for better visibility. Get a bunch of birthday candles and a wad of modeling dough. Using the modeling dough as a base for the candles, stick the candles on her driveway at night, to spell the word "Yes." Quickly light all the candles. Ring her doorbell and run and hide, or honk your horn until she comes out, and then drive off. Beware of wind.

Candy Count

Put several hundred "M&M's" and "Reeses Pieces" candies in a large, clear jar. Count both kinds of candy to ensure that there are a few more "M&M's" than "Reeses Pieces" in the jar. Attach this poem to the top of the jar before delivering it:

> To answer you to the upcoming dance,
> Here's something that'll put you in a trance.
>
> Inside this jar are lots of treats
> For you to count; it's quite a feat.
>
> If there are more 'M&M's' inside of this jar,
> Then my answer is yes, I'll go in your car.
>
> If there are more 'Reeses Pieces' in the jar today,
> Then my answer is no, sorry anyway!
>
> So start that counting, and soon you'll know
> If with you to the dance I plan to go.

Car Scavenger Hunt

Create a scavenger hunt for her that sends her looking all over her car for clues. For example, the first clue might be on her steering wheel; that clue tells her to look on the sun-visor; that clue tells her to look under the passenger seat, etc. The last clue tells her to turn on her cassette player. You have put in a tape which is a recording of your voice saying, "Yes! I'd love to go to the dance with you!"

Caramel Apple

Make him a caramel apple using a green apple. Deliver the caramel apple to him with this message:

> If the apple is green, then I will go,
> But if the apple is red, then the answer is no!"

Chalkboard

Ask a teacher at your school to let you borrow her chalkboard after school. On it, write fifty times on the chalkboard, "I will go to the dance with you!" Afterward, strike up a conversation with the girl who asked you, telling her that you got in trouble in your class that day and that the teacher made you write on the chalkboard as punishment. Ask her to go with you to see if it's still there.

Check Marks

Cut out several check marks from pieces of colored construction paper. Tape them all over his locker. Put a big check mark on the inside of his locker with this message, "CHECK it out! I'd love to go to the dance with you!"

Cheerleaders

At an upcoming sports event, ask the cheerleaders from your school to do a cheer especially for her that answers her to the dance. (Make sure she is going to be at the game.) Or, have a bunch of guys dress up like cheerleaders and do a cheer for her at her doorstep. Here is a sample cheer:

> Hey, (Her name), this is great!
> We've got an answer from your date!
> You asked (Your name) to go with you
> To the (name of dance) dance, and that is true!
>
> He asked us if we would confess,
> His answer to you is Yes, Yes, Yes!

Chewing Gum

Purchase a package of chewing gum. Carefully remove one stick of gum and write on the inside of the gum wrapper, "I CHEWS you over all the others! Yes!" (If you use "Extra" brand chewing gum, add, "We'll have an EXTRA fun time!") Wrap the stick of gum back in its wrapper, insert it back into the package, and give the package of gum to him, or offer him the prepared stick.

Christmas Carol

Revise the words of a Christmas carol to answer him to the dance. For example, use the carol, "Joy To The World," but sing for the opening line, "Joy to the world, he asked me to the dance!" Get a bunch of your friends together and go sing it to him.

Christmas Gifts

Do the Five Days of Christmas (instead of the Twelve Days of Christmas, which is probably too long to wait for an answer) for him. Each day for five consecutive days, leave him a small, anonymous gift such as popcorn or candy, and on the fifth day, accompany the gift with this poem:

> It's the fifth day of Christmas, and so far you've got
> Popcorn and candy, but an answer, you've not!
>
> We've talked to dear Santa, he told us you're good.
> We don't know for a fact, but we trust his word.
>
> But now to the point, good tidings we bring.
> A message for you that will make your heart sing!
>
> The message that we have been sent to deliver
> Has something to do with (Your name)'s Christmas letter.
>
> She wrote to dear Santa to ask if by chance
> She might be your date to the Christmas dance!
>
> Her wish has come true, when you asked her that night,
> Her answer is 'Yes' and to all a good night!

Christmas Lights

One evening when he is at home, arrange a string of Christmas lights on his front lawn so that it spells, "Yes!" Plug in the lights, ring the doorbell, and hide. (Make sure you don't leave the home until he has seen the lights.)

Cinderella

Purchase a high heel shoe from a thrift store, and spray paint it silver. Inside the shoe, insert this message, "I would be as happy as CINDERELLA at the ball, to go to the dance with a HANDSOME PRINCE like you! Yes!" Deliver the shoe to him.

Collage

Search through old magazines and newspapers for articles and advertisements that contain the word "Yes". Cut out as many "Yes"s as you can find and paste them all over a posterboard to create a collage. Tape

ANSWERING WHEN THE ANSWER IS "YES" 53

the posterboard on his ceiling above his bed so that he will see it when he lays down to go to sleep.

Confetti

Cut up colorful pieces of paper into confetti. Using a funnel, pour the confetti into several balloons. Roll up a note which says, "Yes! We'll have a BLAST!" and tuck it inside one of the balloons. Tuck pieces of paper that look like notes in the other balloons to disguise your answer. Blow up the balloons using either helium or air, and deliver them to her. She'll have a colorful surprise when she pops the balloons to find the answer.

Cookie Bouquet

Follow these instructions to make a cookie bouquet: first, get 11 shishkebob sticks. On each one, spear a gumdrop, then a cookie (the chocolate-frosted cookies with a hole in the middle work well for this idea), then another gumdrop. Arrange the sticks in a bouquet by either sticking the stick ends into a piece of styrofoam or by putting all of the sticks into a vase. Put a long-stem red rose in the middle of the cookie-flowers. Inside the rose, insert a little note that says, "Yes!"

Cookie Puzzle

Make a large, hard cookie and write "Yes" in frosting on the cookie. Cut the cookie into puzzle pieces and leave it for him in a box on his doorstep.

Cow

With her parents' permission, take a female cow to her house and tie it to a tree or a post in her front yard. Attach a note to a bell on the cow's neck which reads, "I'd be UDDERLY delighted to go to the dance with you!" Or put, "Have you HERD? The answer is yes!"

Cross Stitch

Cross stitch a simple pattern onto a pillow case. Include the following things on it: his name, your name, the word "Yes", the name of the dance, and the current year. Deliver it to him with a letter which could say, "Just in CASE you were wondering, my answer is yes! I'll be DREAMing about it until we go."

Cupcakes

Make six cupcakes. In the middle of three of them, put a little piece of paper wrapped in plastic: one with a Y, one with an E, and one with an S. Deliver all six cupcakes; he will have to eat all of them to get the answer.

Deodorant
Purchase a stick of "Sure" brand deodorant and give it to her with a note that says, "SURE, no SWEAT! I'm excited to ROLL-ON to the dance with you."

Detectives
Obtain permission from one of his school teachers to take some class time to make an interruption. With a friend or two, dress up as detectives with trench coats, magnifying glasses, and detective hats. During his class, burst open the door and inform the class that you have been investigating to find out who asked you to the dance. State that you are hot on his trail and know that he is in the room. Proceed to give your findings: reveal some facts about him and end up with a description of what he was wearing when he left home this morning. Finally, stare at his face through a magnifying glass. Give him your answer in front of the class.

Dominoes
Ask her parents for permission to use either the kitchen table, the floor, the patio, or the driveway of her home. When she isn't home, set up a "Yes" with dominoes, the larger the better. She can knock it over when she gets home.

Dummy
Make a straw dummy by stuffing some old clothes with straw. Hang it on her front porch or from a tree in her yard. Attach a note to it that says, "I won't leave you HANGING . . . The answer is yes!" Or put, "I'm no DUMMY . . . I'd love to go to the dance with you!"

E-Mail
If he has electronic mail (E-Mail), obtain his E-Mail address and E-mail your answer to him.

Eggs
Give her a dozen eggs. Write one word of this message on each of the eggs, "I'm EGG-cited to go to the dance with you; that's no YOKE!" Put the eggs in order in the egg carton, so she will read the message when she opens the carton.

ANSWERING WHEN THE ANSWER IS "YES"

Electric Fan

Set up an electric fan in her bedroom and turn it on. Attach a card to the fan that says, "You BLOW ME AWAY! Yes, I'd love to go to the dance with you!"

Employer Joke

Ask his employer to call him and say how badly the company needs him to come in to work on the evening of the dance. At the end of the conversation, have the employer say, "Oh, and by the way, (Your name) says yes!" At that time, have the employer confess that he was joking.

Eyelids

Using an eyeliner pencil, write "Yes" on your eyelids. Approach him sometime during the day and make light conversation with him. Then, just before you go, close your eyelids hard for a second or two so he can read your message.

Fax Machine

If she has a fax machine, write your answer on a piece of paper and fax it to her. You might write, "As a matter of FAX, I would love to go with you! Yes!"

Feather

Find or buy a beautiful feather. Mount the feather and this message, written in calligraphy, in a picture frame, "I'd be TICKLED to go to the dance with you." If you go to a zoo and find a flamingo feather, write, "I'd be TICKLED PINK to go to the dance with you!" Gift wrap it and deliver it to him.

Film

Give him a roll of film with this message, "PICTURE this: I like what's DEVELOPING between us. Yes!"

Firecrackers

With her parents' permission, set off some small firecrackers on her front porch. Hang a poster where she will see it that says, "Yes! We'll have a BLAST at the dance together!" Check to see if firecrackers are legal in your state first.

Fish

Using tape that can be removed easily, stick some paper fish of different colors and sizes all over his bedroom wall. On the reverse side of one of the fish, write "Of all the FISHES in the sea, you are the one for me! Yes!"

Fishing Hook

Get a small amount of fishing line and tie a hook on the end of it. Attach a message to the hook that says, "I'm HOOKED, don't you know? It's with you I want to go!" Frame the line, hook, and note in a picture frame for her wall and give it to her.

Fishing Tackle Box

Purchase a small, inexpensive fishing tackle box and place any/all of the following fishing items in it: lead weights, a spinner, a bubble, a swivel, a fly, and salmon eggs. Create a message for him which includes the names of the items in the box. Some ideas: "I can't WEIGHT to go to the dance with you!" "I've been BUBBLEing just thinking about FLYing across the dance floor, SWIVELing my hips and SPINning in circles with you!" "I'm FLOATing on air just thinking about going to the dance with you!" "I'm so EGGcited you asked me!"

Flags

Make or buy small flags of several countries and arrange them in a basket or on a cake. Prepare a card which says "Yes" in as many languages as you can think of and include it in the basket. Some ways to say "Yes" in other languages are "Si" (Spanish and Italian), "Oui" (French), "Da" (Russian), and "Ya" (German).

Flat Tire

Let all the air out of one of the tires on his car. Leave him a pump so he can pump it up again. Attach a note to the pump that says, "I'd FLAT out love to go to the dance with you!"

Flour

Purchase a few five-pound bags of flour from the grocery store. Arrange them in a basket with a card that says, "I bought you some FLOURS to answer you to the dance . . . Yes!"

Flowers

Give her roses and violets with this poem:

Roses are red, violets are blue,
I'd love to go to the dance with you!

Fortune

Give him a fortune cookie which has a message in it that says, "It will be my good FORTUNE to go to the dance with you."

Frisbee

Write a note that says, "I'm excited to SOAR with you at the dance. Yes!" Tape it to the bottom of a frisbee. Take her on a date to the park and play frisbee with her until she finds her answer.

"Froot Loops" Cereal

Give her a box of "Froot Loops" brand cold cereal (make sure it has a picture of the Toucan bird on the box). Insert a note in the cereal box that says, "If any TOUCAN, we can! Yes!"

Gift Box

Fill a box with a hundred or more slips of white paper. Some could be blank, but most of them should say, "Maybe," "Should I?" "I don't know," or "Let me think about it." Include one slip of colored paper which says, "Of course!" Gift wrap the box and give it to her.

Grapes

Fill a basket with bunches of grapes. Deliver it to him with a message that says, "I think you're diVINE, and that going to the dance with you will be GRAPE! You made a HEALTHY choice by asking me. Yes! P.S. See ya 'ROUND."

Gum Balls

Fill an inexpensive gum ball machine with a bunch of different colored gum balls and several small slips of paper. On the slips of paper, write things like, "You BLOW me away! I'd love to go to the dance with you!" "I've been BUBBLING with excitement since you asked me!" "I'm so excited that you CHEWS to go with me to the dance!" "I've liked you ever since you said YELLOW to me and chased away my BLUEs." "I might have to ORANGE my schedule a little, but I'd love to go to the dance with you!" "Your note was the cutest thing I've ever RED, so I'm answering WHITE now: Yes!" "All the other girls will be GREEN with envy that you asked me!"

Hair Dryer

Tape this note to her hair dryer, "You BLEW ME AWAY when you asked me! Yes, I'd love to go to the dance with you!"

Half Time

Answer her at the half-time of a football or basketball game at her high school by getting the announcer to announce your answer over the loudspeakers for you. Or, make a huge banner which has her name and the word "Yes" written on it. During half-time of a school football game or basketball game, when she is nearby, recruit some friends to help you run it across the football field or basketball court.

Hats

Purchase a bunch of inexpensive hats at a thrift store. Hang them all over his bedroom. Leave a sign on his bed that says, "My HAT's off to you . . . Yes!"

Hay And Molasses

Obtain a bail of hay, some molasses, a roll of plastic wrap, and a piece of posterboard. Decorate his car with these ingredients by first covering the car with plastic wrap. Then, spread molasses on the plastic wrap, making sure you don't get any molasses on the car itself. Then, stick hay to the molasses. On top of it all, leave a posterboard that says, "HAY, I'm STUCK on you, SWEETIE. Yes!"

Hay Bales

Put several bales of hay on his doorstep. Stick a large poster to the hay that says, "HAY! I'd love to go to the dance with you!"

"Healthy Choice" TV Dinner

Deliver a "Healthy Choice" brand TV dinner to her with a message on it that says, "Yes is the HEALTHIEST CHOICE I could make!"

Heart Attack

Cut out a bunch of red construction paper hearts and stick them all over her car or bedroom. On one large heart, write, "You gave me a HEART

ANSWERING WHEN THE ANSWER IS "YES"

ATTACK when you asked me to the dance . . . I'd love to go with you!" Or put, "My HEART belongs to you! Yes, I'd love to go!"

Hearts

Cut out 100 red construction paper hearts. Glue each heart to a the top of a popsicle stick. Write "Yes" on 51 of the hearts and "No" on the other 49. At night, push the 100 hearts into his lawn, stick side down. Leave a note on the doorstep that instructs him to find the correct answer by counting the "Yes"s and "No"s. Whichever one is written the most often is your answer.

Horses

Purchase some little plastic toy horses from a convenience store and set them up in his room. Include this note with them, "I won't HORSE around . . . I'd love to TROT with you at the dance!"

"Hot Tamales" Candies

Fill a jar with "Hot Tamales" candies. Stuff a message inside the jar that says, "You are one HOT TAMALE and I'm FIRED UP to go to the dance with you. Yes!"

Ice

Give him a message in a pan of ice that says, "ICE-cept!!!"

Ice Block

Purchase a block of ice from a grocery store. Drill a small hole through the middle of the ice. On a small piece of paper, write, "It will be COOL to go to the dance with you!" Roll the paper in cellophane, stick it in the hole in the ice, and freeze the hole over again by filling it with water and putting the ice block in your freezer. When you give the ice to him, he has to melt the whole block to find his answer.

Ice Cream

Give her a half gallon of ice cream with a card that says, "ICE-CREAM at the chance to go to the dance with you. Yes!"

Ice Cube

Write "Yes" on a little piece of paper and then wrap it in plastic wrap. Freeze the paper inside a cube of ice. Some time after the ice cube has completely frozen, invite your potential date to have a refreshing glass of ice water with you. When you prepare the ice water for both of you, make sure you put the ice cube with the note inside it into his glass. Wait for him to discover it there.

Jack In The Box

Obtain a Jack in the Box toy. Tape a picture of yourself over Jack's face and hang a note around Jack's neck that says, "I just POPPED UP to say yes!" Smash Jack back down into his box, wrap up the box as a gift, and deliver it to her.

Jam

Give him a jar of jam and attach this message, "I'd love to JAM with you at the dance. Yes!"

Jelly Beans

Give him a jar of jelly beans. Include a card that tells him to count the jelly beans for his answer. An even number of jelly beans means "Yes" but an odd number means "No." Make sure you put an odd number of jelly beans in, but include a folded-up note in the jar that says, "Open this after you get your answer." The note tells him, "If you have any question about this answer, see (The name of one of your friends)." When he goes to your friend, demanding an explanation for the "No" answer, she gives him another card. This one reads, "In case of emergency, eat one! Yes!"

"Jolly Ranchers" Candies

Give her a bag of "Jolly Ranchers" wrapped hard candies. Tie a note to the top of the bag that says, "We'll have a JOLLY time at the dance! Yes, I'd love to go with you!"

Landscaping Rock

If his house happens to have colored landscaping rock in the front yard, sneak over at night with a few buckets of landscaping rock of a different color. Lay your rocks down on the colored rocks in his yard to spell "Yes."

Laundry Detergent And T-Shirt

Get a clean, white T-shirt and a bottle of "Yes" brand laundry detergent. Put them together in a basket together with a card that says, "I'm coming CLEAN . . . The answer is yes!"

ANSWERING WHEN THE ANSWER IS "YES"

Laundry Detergent Boxes

Purchase several small boxes of laundry detergent from a laundromat. Arrange them in a basket with a card that uses the brand names of the laundry soap to give him your answer. Some possible sayings are, "I CHEERed when you asked me to the dance!" "The SURF is up! Let's catch the TIDE together, I'd love to go!" "My answer is YES!"

Lawn

Call her parents several days before you answer her and ask them to leave their lawn unmowed until you answer her, so that you can answer her using their lawn. When the time is right, mow "Yes" into the long grass.

Lemon Juice

Dip a Q-Tip in lemon juice, and use it to write "Yes" on a piece of paper. You will not be able to see it when it dries, but when it is placed over heat (such as over but not touching a unit on a stove), the message will appear. Give him the piece of paper with a note that says, "Herein lies your answer, written on this page. To read it, put it over heat, and the message will appear."

Lettuce

Deliver a basket full of heads of lettuce or a salad to his doorstep. Attach a card to the basket which says, "Yes, LETT-UCE go to the dance!"

Locker

Decorate her locker with your answer. Write "Yes" on pieces of paper of all different sizes and colors, and stick them all over the outside and inside of her locker, or just put a big "Yes" on the front of the locker.

"Lucky Charms" Cereal

Purchase a box of "Lucky Charms" brand cold cereal. Carefully slit the bottom of the box open and slide a note inside which says, "Hey CHARMING, today is your LUCKY day. Yes!" Seal the box, place it on his doorstep, ring the doorbell, and run.

"M&M"s Candies

Give him a bag of "M&M"s chocolate candies with a card that reads, "'M&M's won't melt in your hands, but I will at the dance with you! Yes!"

Magnet

Give her a large magnet with a note that reads, "Yes, we'll be the main ATTRACTION at the dance!"

Mail

This answer will take three days for him to receive. On the first day, send him a card in the mail which says, "My Answer . . ." On the second day, send him a card which says, "Is . . ." Finally, on the third day, send him a card which says, "Yes!"

Marbles

Put a bunch of marbles in between the mattress and the fitted sheet of his bed. Include a message with them that reads, "Yes! I'm sure we'll have a MARBLE-ous time at the dance!"

Matches

Glue several matches to a piece of black or red posterboard to form the letters to spell, "You LIGHT up my life! Yes, we'll make the perfect MATCH at the dance!"

Math Problem

Formulate a huge math problem which includes addition, subtraction, multiplication, and division, for which the answer is a positive number. Deliver the math problem to him with a message that tells him to solve it to find your answer. If the answer to the problem is a positive number, then your answer is also positive, but if the answer is a negative number, then your answer is also negative.

Mint

Give her either a mint plant or some breath mints. Write, "I'm not trying to be FRESH, but I think we were MINT to be! I'd love to go to the dance with you!"

Mirror

Give him a small hand mirror with this message attached to it, "IMAGE-ine this: Yes! We'll LOOK great at the dance together!"

Music Notes

Cut several music notes out of black posterboard. Tape them all over her room, and leave this poem on her bed:

ANSWERING WHEN THE ANSWER IS "YES"

I've NOTED that you asked me
To the dance on (day of the week) night.
Your words were MUSIC to my SOUL
And filled me with delight!

It's TIME for me to answer you
And get off of my FEET.
Of course, I'd love to PLAY your TUNE . . .
This date just won't be BEAT!

Oranges

When he is away from home, sneak over to his house and spell "Yes" on his front lawn with a bunch of oranges. You may want to leave a message written on an orange card on one of the oranges that says, "ORANGE you glad I said yes?"

Orchid

Give her an orchid with a card that says, "I won't lie OR-CHID with you . . . Yes!"

Overalls

Give him a pair of overalls with this note pinned to them, "I choose you OVERALL the others. Yes!"

Painted Hearts

Buy some water-based, washable paints that will wash off glass easily. Using the paint, decorate his car windows with hearts. Paint a "Yes" on his windshield and possibly a message that says, "I can HEARTly wait."

Paper Fan

Make a paper fan by taking a piece of paper and folding it back and forth lengthwise into long, thin strips. Staple the bottom of the fan together. Fasten this message to the fan, "I'm your greatest FAN . . . Yes!"

Personal Card

Many stores which sell greeting cards have machines which allow you to create a personalized card with your own message on it. Create an original card for him which gives him your answer to the dance. Send it to him through the mail.

Pick Up Truck

Purchase a small toy pick up truck at a toy store. Using a small amount of hay and some wire or string, make a miniature bale of hay to put in the back of the truck. Place the hay and the truck in a box and include a card which says, "HAY, I'm no easy PICK UP, but you can HAUL me to the dance anytime. Yes!" Deliver the box.

Pie

Cut a circle from a piece of posterboard to fit the exact diameter of the bottom of a pie pan. Write your answer on the circle, laminate it, and place it face up in the bottom of the pie pan. Bake a pie into the pie pan and deliver the pie to him.

Pillow Case Photograph

Buy a pillow case and take it to a store which prints computerized photographs on material. Have the store print a picture of your face on the pillow case. Beneath your picture, write, "Going to the dance with you is a DREAM come true!" Give it to her mother and ask her to slip it onto your date's pillow before she goes to bed that night.

Pink Candy

Purchase a bag of pink candy and tie a card to the bag which says, "I'm tickled PINK to go to the dance with you . . . Yes!" Deliver the candy to him.

Pizza

Make a homemade pepperoni pizza for him. Arrange the pieces of pepperoni on the pizza to spell "Yes." Cook the pizza and deliver it to him hot.

Plastic Forks

Get a bunch of plastic forks and stick them in her lawn in a pattern that spells "Yes."

Plums

Fill a basket with fresh plums. Include this message, "I'd be PLUM tickled to go to the dance with you!"

ANSWERING WHEN THE ANSWER IS "YES"

Pretend "No"

Give him the following poem to make him think your answer is going to be no:

> I feel so very terrible when I have to let you down.
> It tears my heart to pieces and causes me to frown.
>
> The answer 'No' is a bad one, it makes me sick inside.
> Sometimes we all get busy and just want to run and hide.
>
> If this has disappointed you, I'm sorry, as you can guess,
> But don't be sad for long, because my answer to you is 'Yes'!

Pump

Purchase a small ball pump from a sporting goods store. Give it to him with a card that reads, "Yes, I'm PUMPed to go to the dance with you!"

Purse

Give her a purse filled with candy. Put a message inside the purse which says, "Yes! You are the PURSE-on I want to go to the dance with!"

Puzzle

Get a piece of colored cardboard and draw puzzle shapes on it. With a magic marker on the puzzle, write, "It's PUZZLING you didn't ask me sooner. . .Yes!" Cut the cardboard into puzzle pieces, put them in a large bag, and deliver the bag to him.

Restaurant Hunt

Send her on a treasure hunt to several restaurants around town to find your answer. A sample treasure hunt follows:

> *(Clue #1: Leave this at her home)*
> It's getting close to dance time, It's (dance), I'm sure you're aware.
> Before the day gets closer, I'll answer you back—that's fair!
>
> You're going on a treasure hunt, it's the latest trend.
> It's restaurants you will visit, to gather clues to the end.
>
> Follow clues on the cards, doing it with spice,
> Pretty soon you'll have won an answer, 'cause I'm nice!

Here you go, your first clue, home of the Underdog!
The Weinerschnitzel on (address), go there and sing this song:

> 'I wish I were an Oscar Meyer weiner,
> That is what I'd really like to be!
> 'Cause if I were an Oscar Meyer weiner,
> I'd find the clue to see just who likes me!'

(Clue #2: Leave this at Weinerschnitzel)
Nice job, (Her name). But you're not done,
Now a farmer you must be!
Go to McDonald's at (address), and sing this melody:

> 'Old McDonald had a farm, Ee-ii—ee—ii—oo!
> And on that farm he had my clue, Ee-ii—ee—ii—oo!'

(Clue #3: Leave this at McDonald's)
Embarrassed yet? I sure hope not, you carry a tune just great!
Go now to Taco Bell that's here (address)
And chant this song first rate:

> 'La cucaracha, La cucaracha, do you have a clue for me?
> La cucaracha, La cucaracha, may I have it right now please?'

(Clue #4: Leave this at Taco Bell)
Impressive job, you sounded great! Now fake like you are cold,
Go to the Arctic Circle on (address) and sing this to find your gold:

> 'Once there was a snowman, snowman, snowman,
> Once there was a snowman that had my clue!'

(Clue #5: Leave this at Arctic Circle)
Ha ha ha! Thought you were done? Two more to win your prize!
Go to Jack in the Box (address) and sing to make hair rise:

> 'Every night when I come home, the monkey's on the table!
> Give me my clue, or I'll turn blue! Pop goes the weasel!'

(Clue #6: Leave this at Jack in the Box)
It's finally time to get your prize, found in the nearby mall,
Go to TCBY, repeat this rhyme, and you'll be done after all:

> 'My name is (Her name) and I'm here by chance
> To get my answer to the upcoming dance!'

ANSWERING WHEN THE ANSWER IS "YES"   67

(Leave your answer on a piece of paper at this store for the clerk to give her.)

Riddle Hunt

Make up several riddles which, when solved, guide him to a specific location. Write each riddle on a 3" x 5" card and place them all in bottles. Except for the first bottle, which you will give to him personally, bury the bottles in sequence so that the card in the first bottle guides him to the second bottle, and so on. Deliver the first bottle to him with a shovel and instructions that tell him to figure out the riddle, go to the place where the riddle sends him, and then hunt for the "X" at that location. When he finds the "X," he is to dig beneath it until he finds another bottle with a riddle in it. This bottle will lead him to the next "X." He is to continue this way until he comes to the final "X." At the final "X," place a bottle with a note inside it that says, "Yes!"

"Rit" Dye

Purchase a small box of "Rit" clothing dye and tie a note to it that says, "It's been RIT-ten: I'm DYE-ing to go to the dance with you! Yes!" Give it to her.

Rock And Pillow

Find a smooth, fist-sized rock and paint "Yes" on it. Give it to his mother and ask her to place it underneath his pillow before he goes to bed that night.

Rolling Pin

Tie a card to a rolling pin that says, "I won't FLATTEN your hopes . . . Yes! I'd love to go to the dance with you!" Deliver the rolling pin to her.

Rose

Give him a rose with this message, "I finally ROSE to the occasion . . . Yes! I'd love to go to the dance with you!"

Rose In Ice

Buy a red rose and clip the stem so that the rose is short enough to fit sideways into a five-gallon ice cream bucket. Write your answer on the inside of a card, laminate the card, and attach the card to the rose. Carefully pour enough water into the bucket to generously cover the rose.

If you choose, you can tie fishing line to the rose and both edges of the bucket to suspend the rose and keep it from touching the sides or bottom of the bucket. Place the bucket in your freezer until its contents are frozen solid. Remove the solid block of ice from the bucket and deliver it to her doorstep. Ring the doorbell and run.

Roses

For a simple, romantic answer, deliver some long-stem red roses to her. On an attached card, write, "Yes!"

Sailboat

Fill his bathtub with water. Arrange some rocks on the bottom of the bathtub so that they spell "Yes." Float a toy sailboat on top of the water, and leave a message in the sailboat which says, "I've been SAILING ever since you asked me!"

Scented Candle

Deliver a scented candle to her with a letter that says, "It makes SCENTS that I say yes, because you LIGHT up my life!"

Scissors

Give him a pair of scissors. Tie a message to the handle that says, "You're a real CUT-UP! Yes, an evening with you at the dance will be SHARP!"

"Scope" Mouthwash

Purchase a bottle of "Scope" brand mouthwash. Tie a note to the bottle which says, "I've been SCOPING you out for some time. You took my BREATH away when you asked me to the dance . . . Yes!"

"Sees" Chocolates

Get a box of "Sees" brand chocolate candies. Gift wrap the box and send it to him with a card that says, "I'm SEESing this SWEET opportunity to go to the dance with you. Yes!"

Serenade

If you are brave and are gifted in the theatrical arts, arrange with a teacher of one of her classes to take just a few minutes during class to answer her. At the appointed time, burst into the classroom, kneel before her, and serenade her. Either write your own song that answers her to the dance or find a good, romantic song that talks about wanting to be together. When your song is over, leave her a rose and a card that says, "Yes!"

Shaved Head

If you feel crazy enough, have the hair shaved off your head except for a fuzzy "Yes." It shouldn't take too long for your reply to be noticed.

Shoe

Go to a thrift store and purchase a pair of shoes your size that have good, thick soles on them. Carefully carve "Yes" into the sole of one of the shoes. Carve it deep enough and big enough that it will leave an impressive imprint as you walk through snow or mud. To answer her, simply walk with her through the snow or mud. You may want to say to her something like, "Oh, by the way, I wanted to tell you something about the way you asked me to the dance. That's all BEHIND US now." Glance backwards toward your tracks, and hopefully she will too. If she doesn't, just pretend like you stepped on a nail and tell her that you need her to check the bottom of your shoe to see if she can pull it out.

Short Sheet

Sneak over to his house and short-sheet his bed. Leave him a note near the foot of his bed underneath the sheets which says, "In SHORT, Yes!"

"Smarties" Candies

Ask her mom to lay a pair of her pants out on her bed. Buy a bunch of "Smarties" wrapped candies, unwrap several packages of them, and leave an obvious trail of "Smarties" from her front door to her bedroom and then to the pair of pants. Stick wrapped packages of "Smarties" all over her pants so that they are visibly hanging out of pockets, belt loops, and leg cuffs. Inside one of the pants pockets, place a card that says, "Yes, SMARTIE PANTS! I'd love to go to the dance with you!"

Smiley Faces

Cut different sized circles out of several pieces of yellow posterboard. With a black magic marker, draw smiley faces on each circle. Tape them all over his bedroom, on his bed, dresser, walls, door, and window, for example. Leave him a sign that says, "I'm all SMILES . . . Yes, I'd love to go to the dance with you!"

Smoke Bomb

Put a small smoke bomb on her front doorstep next to a note that says, "Yes! We'll have a SMOKIN' time at the dance!" Light the smoke bomb, ring the doorbell, and hide.

Snow

If it's winter and if there's lots of snow on the ground, go to his house and stomp "yes" in the snow.

Snowmen

If there is a lot of snow in her front yard, build a snowman and a snow woman dancing together. Put a sign in one of their hands that says, "Yes!"

Soap Window

Sneak over to his house at night and write "Yes" on either his bedroom window or his car window with soap that will wash off easily.

Socks In Car

Go to a thrift store and buy a few dozen socks. They don't even need to match. Spread the socks either all over the inside of his car or all over his bedroom. Put a message inside one of the socks that says, "You knock my SOCKS off . . . Yes! I will go to the dance with you!"

Socks In Drawer

Buy a pair of socks. Put a little note inside of them, so that it is partially showing. The note says, "Yes, we'll make a great PAIR at the dance!" Ask her mother to put them in her sock drawer.

"Spaghetti-O" Roulette

Send him a can of "Spaghetti-Os" and a note instructing him to open the can and count each "Spaghetti-O." If the number comes out even, then your answer is "Yes," but if the answer comes out odd, then the your answer is "No." After he has been counting for about twenty minutes, have someone either call him or deliver him another note which says, "If you need to eat one 'Spaghetti-O,' please do . . . My answer is 'Yes'!"

Spots

Cut out different colored and different sized circles and tape them all over his room with tape that can be removed easily. On one of the circles, write, "I'm so excited, I'm seeing SPOTS! Yes!"

Stars

Purchase some glow-in-the-dark adhesive stars from a toy store. Arrange them on top of his bedroom ceiling so that they spell "Yes." Then, leave a message on his pillow that says, "Look to the STARS for your answer to the dance."

Styrofoam Locker

Fill her locker with packing Styrofoam by following these instructions: open the locker. Tape plastic wrap over the front of the locker except for a small hole at the top. Pour the Styrofoam in the locker through the hole, close the locker, and pull the plastic wrap out the side of the locker. Write this message on a piece of paper and include it with the Styrofoam, "Life would be a MESS if I couldn't go to the dance with you . . . Yes!" When she opens her locker, all the Styrofoam and the message will come flying out.

Sugar

Put some sugar in a jar or purchase a few small bags of sugar and arrange them in a basket. Attach a note that says, "Hey SUGAR, it was SWEET of you to ask me! Yes!"

"Sunny Delight" Drink

Give her a bottle of "Sunny Delight" citrus drink. Tie a card to the bottle that says, "Hey SUNNY, I'd be DELIGHTED to go to the dance with you! Yes!"

Suntan

Have a friend write, "Yes" with sun block on your back. Then, go outside on a hot day and lay out in the sun. Get your back tan . . . except for the sun blocked message. When you see your potential date, show her your back to give her your answer. If you're afraid sun block won't create enough of a contrast, cut the letters "Y," "E," and "S" out of a piece of posterboard and tape them to your back before laying in the sun.

T-Shirt

Purchase a white T-shirt in his size. Using washable markers, write several phrases on the T-shirt like, "Yes," "No," "Maybe," "Absolutely Not," "I'd Love To," "Not On Your Life," and "Of Course" all over the T-shirt. Using a permanent marker, write one "Yes" on the T-shirt. Deliver the T-shirt to him with instructions that tell him your answer is on the shirt. After a few minutes, deliver a message to him that says, "Answer after washing!" After he washes it, only the permanent answer will remain.

Taco

Make him a plate of homemade tacos. Inside one of the tacos, insert a note wrapped in plastic that says, "Yes, I'd love TA-CO with you!" Deliver them hot.

Tags

Buy some fluorescent price tags and tie them all over his bedroom. Number twelve of the tags one through twelve. On each of the twelve numbered tags, write one word of this message, "Yes, I would love to TAG along with you at the dance."

Tanning Oil

Give her a bottle of tanning oil. Tie a note to the top of the bottle that says, "OIL be glad to go to the dance with you . . . We'll have a fan-TAN-stic time!"

Telephone Book

Highlight a bunch of "Y"s and "N"s in a phone book, making sure to mark a few more "Y"s than "N"s. Deliver the phone book to her with a message on it which indicates that she is to count the highlighted "Y"s and "N"s. If there are more "Y"s, the answer is yes, but if there are more "N"s, the answer is no.

Toilet Paper

Spread "Charmin" brand toilet paper all over his bedroom or his car. Write him a message on toilet paper that says, "Yes, we'll have a CHARMIN' time together at the dance! I'd love TOILET you take me!"

Toilet Plunger And "Almond Joy" Candy Bar

Purchase a toilet plunger and tape an "Almond Joy" brand chocolate candy bar on it. Tie this note to the handle of the plunger, "I would be OVER-JOYED to go to the dance with you. Yes!"

ANSWERING WHEN THE ANSWER IS "YES"

Toothpaste

On the tiniest piece of paper you can fit it on, write, "ALL WHITE! I'll go to the dance with you!" Laminate the paper and then roll it up small enough to fit into a tube of toothpaste. Slide it into the tube, pushing it just far enough inside that it is hidden but that it will come out with the next squeeze. Deliver the tube of toothpaste to his house when he is not there, asking his mother to place it in his bathroom near his toothbrush.

"Total" Brand Cereal

Using a razor blade, carefully slice a thin slit in the top of a "Total" brand cold cereal box. Slide a note inside the box that says, "My life has been TOTAL happiness since you asked me to the dance .. Yes! I would love to go to the dance with you!" Wrap the cereal box up as a present and deliver it to him for breakfast.

Treasure Chest

Fill a small treasure chest full of pennies. On the back of one of the pennies, tape a little piece of paper that says, "Yes." Bury the treasure chest somewhere in his backyard. Create a scavenger hunt with clues that send him hunting all over until he finally finds the buried treasure. In the chest, place instructions that one of the pennies contains the answer.

Trench Coat

Find out when the person who asked you to the dance is going to be in a public setting such as a school sports event or an assembly. Have a friend dress up with a trench coat, hat, and sunglasses and approach her. After getting her attention, he flashes open the flap of his trench coat to reveal a large "Yes" pinned to his shirt. Then, he quickly walks away.

Video

Rewind a video all the way to the beginning of the tape. Simultaneously start a timer and begin playing the video. View the video until one of the characters states the word "yes". Stop the timer and write down the exact amount of time the video had been playing until the word "yes" was said, as near to the second as possible. Rewind the video again. Deliver it to him with a message that states that the answer is found in the video. Tell him the exact amount of time he must watch the video until the answer is given.

Watch

Give him a watch and a card that reads, "WATCH out! You're in for a really great TIME every SECOND of this dance! I just love your FACE, so get in GEAR for a great evening! Yes, I'd love to go to the dance with you!"

Water On Door

Put a plastic cup of water on top of his barely opened bedroom door. When he opens the door, the water should fall off the door and splash him on the head. Tape this note to the cup, "WATER you waiting for? We'll have a BIG SPLASH at the dance! Yes!"

Wax Paper

Sneak over to his house at night and spell out a big "Yes" on his front lawn with a roll of wax paper. Weight it down either with rocks or with small sticks pushed through the wax paper into the lawn.

Weeds

For a group answer, gather a bunch of weeds and give them to the people asking you. Include a card that says, "WEED love to go to the dance with you!"

Wheat

For a group answer, get a small container of wheat and give it to the people asking you. Include a card that says, "WHEAT love to go to the dance with you!"

Wigs

Go to a thrift store and purchase a bunch of old, inexpensive wigs. Put them all over his car. Leave a poster on his windshield that says something like, "I've been WIGging out ever since you asked me! HAIR I come! Yes!"

Window

Have a friend dress up as a private detective and deliver a secret message to his house. The message says, "TOP SECRET: for your answer, drive by my house tonight at 10:00 p.m. If one candle is burning in my bedroom window, the answer is no. If three candles are burning in my window, the answer is yes." Burn three candles in your window that night at 10:00 p.m.

Windshield

Early one frosty morning, drive to her house before she leaves for the day and scrape "Yes" on her frost-covered car windshield with an ice scraper.

Yeast

Give him a bag of yeast. Attach this message to the bag, "Yes, it's the YEAST I could do to go to the dance with you!"

Zoo Scavenger Hunt

Prepare a scavenger hunt throughout your local zoo using words from animal information plaques to spell out your answer. The answers to the clues, when put together in order, spell out, "Yes, I would love to go to the dance with ZOO!" (For example, Clue #1 could read, "Black Bears, Line 7, Word 2," if that word is "yes"). Give her a pre-paid ticket to your local zoo and attach the clues of the scavenger hunt to the ticket. She must go to the zoo, find the correct animal information plaques, and write down the correct words to get your answer.

Chapter Three

Answering When The Answer Is "No"

Air Freshener

Give her a can of air freshener with this poem attached to it:

My answer really STINKS because it is no,
I've got some other plans and I just can't go.
But maybe we could try something after this dance
When the AIR is clear and we have a FRESH chance.

Army Tank

Buy him a couple of toy army tanks and deliver them to him. Include a card which says, "TANKS for asking, but my answer is no."

"Band Aids" Adhesive Strips

Stick a bunch of "Band Aids" adhesive strips all over a large piece of posterboard. On the poster, write, "I wish this was an OUCHless answer, but I'm HURT to say that I can't go to the dance with you!"

Beans

Give her a can of beans with this message, "Sorry, but I've already BEAN asked!"

Beef Jerky

Give him a canister of beef jerky with a card that says, "I feel like such a JERK, but someone else asked me BEEFore you! Think of me, though, next time your weekend looks DRY."

ANSWERING WHEN THE ANSWER IS "NO"

Bookmark

Make a bookmark for her that says, "Sorry, but I'm BOOKED that night! MARK me down for another occasion!" Put the bookmark in one of her books where she is sure to find it.

Bullet

Glue a bullet to a note that says, "SHOOT, I can't go to the dance with you!"

Cactus

Give him a cactus plant with this message tied to it, "I hate to DESERT you . . . this has been PRICKING my conscience for quite a while, but I can't STICK with you at the dance! Sorry!"

Can And Knot

Tie a piece of rope in a knot around a can of soda pop. Fasten this message to the can, "I'm sorry, but I CAN KNOT go to the dance with you." Deliver it to her.

Candy Hearts

Take the paper prescription off of an old prescription canister, wash out the canister well, and fill it with candy hearts. Type up a new prescription and tape it to the canister. The new prescription could say something like:

> In case of mild heartache, take two per hour.
> In case of more severe heartache, take four per hour.
> If symptoms persist after the prescription is gone,
> Call (your phone number) for a date and a heart check.

Deliver this prescription to him with a letter that explains that you can't go to this dance with him, that you'd like to go out with him in the future, and that you ordered him this prescription in case of any heartache.

Caramel Apple

Send him some caramel apples with a card that says, "Sorry about this STICKY mess, but I can't go to the dance with you this time."

"Chapstick" Lip Balm

Purchase a tube of "Chapstick" lip balm and give it to him with the following poem:

> I hope you're not CHAPPED
> But I have to say 'No,'
> But STICK around, please,
> And next time we'll go!

Coupon

Create a coupon which entitles him to a future date with you. Send it to him with a card that explains that you can't go to the dance with him this time, but that he can use the coupon to take you to a future dance. Send the coupon to him in the mail.

Crab Meat

Deliver a package of crab meat to her. Attach this message to it, "I hate to be a CRAB, but my answer is no. Maybe we could MEAT up with each other another time."

Crushed Ice

If you are already dating someone else, give him a bag of crushed ice. Staple a card to it that says, "I'm CRUSHED to say no, but I'm in COLD STORAGE right now!"

Deodorant

Purchase some deodorant and give it to her with the following message, "Sorry, this is the PITS and it really STINKS, but I have to say no this time!"

Dessert

Prepare a plate which contains a few different desserts such as cupcakes, brownies, and cookies. Wrap the plate of food in plastic wrap and deliver it to her with a note which says, "I hate to DESSERT you for this dance, but I've already got plans. It was SWEET of you to ask!"

Doughnuts

Purchase a box of a dozen doughnuts. Write the following message on a card and attach it to the box, "I've thought about it a DOZEN times, but I DOUGHNUT think I can go with you to the dance! Sorry!" Deliver the box to him.

ANSWERING WHEN THE ANSWER IS "NO"

Dump Truck

Deliver a toy dump truck to him that has a bunch of candies in the back of it. Stuff a card inside the candies which says, "I hate to DUMP this on you, but I'm already TRUCKing to the dance with someone else."

Facial Tissue

Give him a box of facial tissue with the following message tucked inside the dispenser, "I just can't go to the dance with you . . . I'm too WIPED out!"

Fake Hand

Buy a fake hand from a costume store. Gift wrap it and deliver it to him with this message, "My HAND has already been taken for this dance, but please accept this one as a rain check, until we can go out some other time."

Fir Stud

Obtain a Hem Fir stud (often just called a "two by four") from a lumber yard. Deliver it to him with a message on it which declines his invitation. The message might include any/all of the following phrases: "I hate to go against the GRAIN and say no, but I can KNOT go with you to this dance." "I wish you WOOD have asked me sooner." "Don't LUMBER around and get WARPED about this, because I WOOD love to do something else with you another time." "Who WOOD KNOT want a date with such a STUD like you? Call me after the dance and I'll treat you to a MILL. I promise you won't be BOARD."

Fishing Hook

Give her some fishing line with a hook on the end, all tangled up into a big snag. Attach a note that says, "I'd fall for you HOOK, LINE, and SINKER . . . but someone else already SNAGGED me for the dance! Sorry!"

Fishing Reel

Give him a fishing reel, some fishing line, and a fishing hook. On the end of the hook, attach this message, "I'd REELy like to go to the dance with you, but I've already been HOOKED!"

French Fries

Deliver a box of french fries to him with this message, "I wish I could go to the dance with you, but I'm just too FRIED!"

Garbage Can

Purchase a small garbage can. Put a message in it that says, "I feel like GARBAGE, but I can't WASTE another minute . . . I can't go with you this time! I already have a HEFTY night planned."

Geode

Give him a geode with a note that says, "GEODE love to go to the dance with you, but I'm ROCKing with someone else that night. I want to be OPEN with you and make something CRYSTAL clear . . . I would love to do something with you in the future!"

"Gummy Worms" Candies

Deliver a can of "Gummy Worms" gummy candies to him with a note which says, "I'm not trying to WORM my way out of this, but I've already been CHEWsen by someone else for the dance."

Honey

Purchase a little bottle of honey and give it to him with the following poem:

> Sorry, HONEY, but I'm as busy as a BEE.
> Maybe next dance, though, you can go with me!

Horse Shoe

Deliver a horse shoe to him with this message, "I won't HORSE around with you. My answer is NAY . . . Someone else grabbed my REINS for this dance! But here is a HORSE SHOE to remind you that I hope I'll be LUCKY enough to do something with you in the future!"

Ice Cream Bars

Purchase a box of ice cream bars and slip the following note inside the box before delivering it to his house, "Sorry for the COLD answer, but I can't go to the dance with you. ICE CREAM with delight if you'd ask me out another time."

"Jello"

Give him a glass dish of "Jello". Underneath the dish, facing upwards, tape the following message, "I'm SET in my ways and can't go to the dance with you. Maybe we could CHILL together another time." Deliver it to him.

ANSWERING WHEN THE ANSWER IS "NO"   81

"Lemon Drops" Candies

Buy him a box of "Lemon Drops" sour candies. Present them to him with a note which says, "I hate to be a SOUR LEMON, but I can't go to the dance with you. Please DROP me a line some other time for a SWEETER answer."

Mad Magazine

Insert a flyer into a copy of *Mad* magazine that says, "I'm really MAD about this, but I can't go with you to the dance!" Give the magazine to her.

Mummy

Follow these instructions to make a mummy: first, make a dummy by stuffing some old clothing with straw. Then, completely wrap the dummy in toilet paper or strips of an old sheet. Pin a note to the mummy that says, "I'm sorry I can't go this time . . . I'm all WRAPPED UP!" Leave the mummy on his front doorstep.

Newspaper

Give her today's newspaper with a note that says, "I have some bad NEWS . . . I can't go to the dance with you!"

Peanut Butter

Purchase a jar of peanut butter and attach this card, "I'm sorry, but I'm in a STICKY situation and I can't go to the dance with you! You'd BUTTER try next time!"

"Pick Up Sticks"

Buy a canister of "Pick Up Sticks" from a toy store. Gift wrap it and deliver it with a letter that says, "Sorry, but I'm not going be STICKing around for the dance. I would love it if you'd PICK ME UP for another time!"

Potpourri

Deliver a package of potpourri to her with a card that reads, "I don't want to LEAF you hanging without an answer, BUD someone else already SNIFFED me out for this dance. SCENTS you asked, I'd love to go out with you another time."

Present

Put this note in a small box, "I'm sorry, but I'm all WRAPPED up that evening! Can I request your PRESENTS for the next dance?" Gift wrap the box and deliver it to her.

Rocks And Rolls

Fill a basket with some washed rocks and some homemade rolls. Attach the following message, "I would love to ROCK and ROLL with you at the dance, but I can't go with you this time. BUTTER keep me in mind for next time, DOUGH. Until then, save your BREAD."

Rope

Put a long piece of rope on her doorstep. Fasten a note to the end of the rope that reads, "Sorry, I can KNOT go to the dance with you. I'm all TIED UP!"

Rubber Bands

Give him a bunch of rubber bands with this message, "I hope this isn't STRETCHING it, but I've been BANDED by someone else for this FLING. Please save me for another SHOT."

Shapes

Cut several different shapes out of construction paper: squares, circles, triangles, and rectangles. Decorate his room with them and write this message on one of the shapes, "Sorry to be such a SQUARE, but I'm in no SHAPE to go to the dance! Maybe we can TRI-AN-GLE together next time!"

Shoes

Go to a thrift store and purchase a bunch of old, inexpensive shoes. Tie them to a long, heavy string and tie the string to his bedroom door. On one of the shoes, attach this message, "My SOLE wants to go, but my parents said no!"

Shorts

Purchase a pair of shorts for him. Deliver them in a box with a card that says, "Sorry, but I just can't go with you on such SHORT notice. Maybe next time."

ANSWERING WHEN THE ANSWER IS "NO"

Sink
Put a sign under her kitchen sink which says, "I hate to have to LEAK the answer to you this way, but I can't go to the dance with you. I feel like such a DRIP! Maybe we could get FIXED UP some other time." Leave her a clue in her bedroom for her to search for the answer in her kitchen.

Soap
Give her a bar of soap and this poem:

> Thank you for asking, but I better come CLEAN:
> I can't go to dances till I turn sixteen!

Spanish Answer
Deliver a note to him that says, "I didn't want to hurt your feelings, so I decided to answer you in Spanish: No."

String
Tie one long string to several objects in her bedroom. Leave a note that says, "Sorry, but I'm all STRUNG up for this dance already!"

Sweet And Sour Dinner
Cook him a meal that uses sweet and sour sauce. Deliver it to his house with a card that says, "I have a SWEET AND SOUR message for you: I can't go to this dance with you, but I was wondering if you would go to the next dance with me!"

Teddy Bear
Send her a stuffed teddy bear with a note in its arms that says, "I can BEARly bring myself to say it, but I can't go to the dance with you, because my evening is already STUFFED!"

Ties
Buy two ties at a thrift store. Tie them loosely around your neck and then slip them off, so that they are properly tied with knots in them. Deliver them to him with a card that says, "I feel so KNOTTY, but I have to say no because I'm 2 TIED up that evening."

Time Magazine

Give him a current *Time* magazine with a flyer inserted into it that says, "Sorry, but I can't go with you this TIME."

Weiner

Make her a gourmet hot dog with all the trimmings. Attach a note to it that says something like, "I hope you won't think I'm a WEINER, but I've already BUN CHEWsen by someone else. Please KETCHUP with me after the dance, though, because I would RELISH a date with you!"

Chapter Four

Ideas For Dinner

Boating Banquet

Take your date to a nice boat docked nearby (or just sitting in your driveway). Have dinner in the cabin or on the bow, with a younger brother or sister dressed as a waiter or waitress, ready to serve you. A seafood dinner would be appropriate for this setting.

Campfire Cookout

Prior to the dance, set up a tent and a small campfire in your backyard. For dinner, take your date in the backyard and cook dinner with her over the campfire. Your meal could consist of tin foil dinners, which are made by filling sheets of aluminum foil (shiny side in) with vegetables such as carrots, potatoes, and onions. Add a raw hamburger patty seasoned with whatever you like, and wrap the aluminum foil completely around the meal. Place the dinners into the hot coals of your campfire and listen to them sizzle as they cook. Turn them every few minutes and check them frequently until the ingredients inside are completely cooked. A good dessert to go with this dinner would be S'mores, which are made by roasting a marshmallow over the campfire and placing it and a square of a chocolate candy bar in between two graham crackers. When your meal is ready, eat inside your tent.

Cheap-O Surprise

For this group date to the dance, tell your dates that you've spent so much money on the dance that you can't afford an expensive meal. Drive to a fast food restaurant and have someone in your party go in and pick up one hamburger and ask for a bunch of extra sacks, which she then proceeds to make look like they're full of food. When she returns to the car, tell the group that you're going to go back to your house to eat it. Upon arrival at your house, and to the surprise (and relief) of your dates, you find a feast of steaks, shrimp, or other fancy meal that you have pre-arranged waiting for you on the table.

Chinese Dinner

Purchase Chinese food from a take-out Chinese restaurant, and take it to a park or other romantic setting. Don't forget the chopsticks!

Coded Dinner

Invite a few couples over for dinner at your home. Assign each couple to bring a specific type of food. Before the date, make a menu for each person in the group. These menus should offer several different foods, each written in code form. (For example: "Italian worms" = spaghetti; "chopped up heads" = a dinner salad; "pronghorn" = a fork; "buttercup" = a drinking glass.) When your guests arrive, seat them and offer them their menus. Have them order by code, and then serve them whatever they ordered. Depending on the order, you or your date could end up with all food and no silverware, or all silverware and no food!

Dinner On The Go

For a "moving" experience, eat your dinner on a train. Purchase round trip tickets to a nearby city, and enjoy the scenery and the experience as you eat in the dining compartment of the train. A less expensive version of this idea can be done by eating dinner in a motor home, with a driver and a waiter to serve you.

Good Grazing

Prepare a candlelight dinner in the middle of a field. Use a cellular phone to call your waiter (a family member or friend) who is waiting for you in a nearby house or car. Place your order, play romantic music, and wait for your dinner to arrive.

Homemade Pizzas

Purchase in advance all of the ingredients for delicious pizzas. With your group, make the pizza dough and sauce, and then smother it with all of your favorite ingredients. To make things interesting, you might

IDEAS FOR DINNER 87

add some limitations such as blindfolding some of the couples and tying the hands together of other couples.

Kidnapped Dates

Take your group to a less expensive, less impressive restaurant. After being seated, excuse yourself to visit the men's room. On the way, find your waitress and inform her that you won't really be eating here, and request her help in your plans (slip her a tip). After a few moments, the other young men excuse themselves to check on you to see what is taking you so long. You never return to the table. After a few minutes, your waitress approaches the ladies and informs them that their dates have just been kidnapped. She hands them a ransom note which you have given her beforehand that instructs the ladies to track you down. Included also with the note is Clue #1. Clue #1 leads them outside to a car and a hidden key. Inside the car is Clue #2, which leads them to the first location of a chase to find you. Make up as many clues as you want, depending on the time you want them to take to search for you. Meanwhile, you and the other guys have sped away in a truck which contains a barbecue grill and all the fixings for a great barbecue dinner. Drive to the final location of the chase, set up the grill, begin fixing dinner, and wait for your dates to find you.

Moving Van Supper

Have everyone in your group meet at a school parking lot and eat dinner in the back of a parked moving van which you have rented for the evening. Make sure you get clearance from the moving company for this idea before renting the van.

Pickup Picnic

Pick up your date for dinner before the dance in a pickup truck. Make a detour from the route to the restaurant, however, and head to a romantic, secluded spot. When you arrive at your designated spot, pretend you have a flat tire, and get out to have a look. Tell your date that it looks bad, so you'll just have to eat here. Then, in the bed of the truck, quickly set up a small table and two folding chairs. Cover the table with a tablecloth and place a candle, silverware, glasses, and plates on top of it. Reach inside the cab and turn on some romantic music. Bring out a hot dinner, which you have kept in a warmer, and serve your date dinner in the back of the truck.

Progressive Dinner

For this group dinner, eat appetizers at one person's house, soup and salad at another person's house, the main dish at yet another person's house, and finally, dessert at the final person's house.

San Francisco Supper

Invite everyone to your house for dinner. Plan a meal that is potentially messy and potentially difficult to eat. Seat your guests at a table which is set with everything necessary to eat except for silverware. Have each person choose a number out of a hat. Then, bring out a tray on which are several kitchen utensils such as potato mashers, wire whisks, tongs, and spatulas. Each utensil has a number on it. Help your guests find their utensils by matching the numbers they drew from the hat to the same numbered utensils on the tray. The couples then put on huge bibs (towels) and eat their dinner using their selected utensils. To make things really interesting, have each person try to feed her date.

Silver Platter TV Dinners

Prior to the dance, have all the guys go shopping and purchase TV dinners for themselves and their dates. Heat them and hide them from the girls under fancy silver platters. The guys tell their dates that they have worked all day cooking a fancy silver platter dinner for them. When everyone is seated at the table, which the guys have elegantly decorated with fine china, a lace tablecloth, and candles, bring out the covered silver platters, set them on the table, take the lids off, and, to the ladies' surprise, reveal the TV dinners.

Slides Of Baby Photographs

For this group date, go to your house for dinner where a delicious meal will be served. While waiting to be served dinner, mention that you have some entertainment planned. Direct everyone's attention toward the television set, and watch the emotion in your dates' faces as they discover that the entertainment is a collection of their baby slides which you have previously collected from their parents. Watch the slides while you eat your meal.

Synchronized Spaghetti Sucking

Bring everyone to your house for a spaghetti dinner. Seat everyone around a large table and serve everyone a large helping of spaghetti.

IDEAS FOR DINNER

Synchronize the dinner by connecting your guests' hands with a tight string so that they all have to lift their forks to their mouths at the same time in order to eat.

Wild West

Prepare wild game for dinner. Dig out your favorite recipe for elk, venison, antelope, turkey, duck, goose, pheasant, trout, bass, catfish, or whatever wild meat you have access to. You may want to give your date a menu in advance to let her choose what would be most to her liking. Serve the wild game with wild fruits and vegetables such as blackberries and water cress salad with bottled spring water. For dessert, serve Indian fry bread with fresh honey.

Winner Dinner

For this group dinner, one member of each couple prepares a dinner for two. The dinners should be full meals which each include an appetizer, a salad, a main course, dessert, and a beverage. The chefs should cover their meals so that the food cannot be seen, and they might keep their meals hot by putting them in a warmer. For the dinner, when everyone is together, sit down to the table and display the covered meals. Before eating, play a short game such as charades. Whoever wins the first round gets the first choice of which mystery meal he would like he and his date to eat for dinner. Continue playing rounds of the game until all of the meals have been chosen. When everyone is ready to eat, pass out silverware, uncover your meals, and enjoy your surprise dinners.

World Traveler Cuisine

Plan dinner at your house. Prepare an appetizer which is from one country, soup from a second country, the main course from a third country, and dessert from a fourth country. Serve the appetizer in one room. Then, play a cassette tape of an airplane taking off, and announce that you have just landed in the next country. Get up and walk into a different room where the next course is waiting. Continue in this pattern until you have traveled to the four different countries.

Chapter Five

After-The-Dance Activities

Advertising Agents

Obtain several different household products such as a flyswatter, hair spray, liquid soap, and a toaster, and lay them on a table. Make sure you have at least one product per couple. Assign each product a number, and number several slips of paper and put them in a hat. Each couple chooses a number out of the hat and finds its corresponding household product. For the next ten or fifteen minutes, each couple prepares an advertisement for its selected product. The advertisement could be a dialogue, a skit, a song, or a combination of these. After the time is up, the couples take turns presenting their advertisements to the other couples. After all the participants have had their turns performing, let them vote which product they would be most tempted to buy after viewing its advertisement.

Cardboard Car Drive-in

Have everyone in your group meet at your house after the dance, where you have previously collected supplies such as large cardboard boxes, magic markers, construction paper, and flashlights. Each couple must make a car out of a cardboard box and the other supplies your have provided, and then "drive" it into your living room when it is completed. Have someone judge the cars to select a winning couple. The winners have to pop popcorn for the others. When the popcorn is ready, put in a video, climb into your "cars," and watch the show at your homemade drive-in movie theater.

AFTER-THE-DANCE ACTIVITIES

Charades

Have someone not involved in this game write several words or phrases that would be fun and challenging to act out on slips of paper. Place the slips of paper into a hat and divide all the couples into two teams. Each couple chooses a slip of paper from the hat, brainstorms together for sixty seconds on how to effectively act out its word or phrase so that its teammates can guess what it is, and then silently acts out its word or phrase to the members of its team.

Dictionary Game

For this game, each person will need paper and a pencil or pen. One person finds a word in the dictionary that no participant is familiar with. He announces the word, and everyone writes it down on his paper. Next to it, each person writes down a possible definition that he makes up, which he thinks will fool the other players. The person with the dictionary writes down the true definition of the word on his paper. The person with the dictionary collects the definitions, shuffles them, and then reads them out loud. Each player must select the definition he or she thinks is correct and cast his vote secretly. If no one selects the correct definition, the person who chose the word gets one point. Anyone who selects the correct definition scores one point. Anyone who fooled another with his made up definition receives one point for each person he fooled. After the first round, the dictionary rotates to another player who selects the next word.

Finger Paint Pictionary

Play this game like normal Pictionary, except use finger paints and butcher paper instead of pencil and paper to draw the pictures. Hang the completed paintings on the wall to dry and to display your creative art gallery. Pudding can be used instead of finger paints if you want to lick your fingers clean after each drawing.

Gotcha

Each person needs either squirt gun or a squirt bottle for this activity. Meet together inside a large building such as a warehouse or a school building, or play outdoors. Divide into two teams. Members of each team should wear white T-shirts and fill their squirt bottles with a different color of water so they can tell when they get hit by a member of the opposite team. The goal is to squirt members of the opposite team but to avoid getting squirted by them. Each team starts on a different side of the playing area, but at the sound of a whistle they begin pursuing each other. This game can also be played by trying to capture the other team's flag, which is located somewhere on its side, or it can be played in the dark if team members carry flashlights.

Homemade Movies

With all of the couples together, write a script for a short movie in which all of you have acting parts. Assign roles, find and dress up in simple costumes, choose filming locations, and then, using a home video camera, go to the selected locations and make your movie. When you're finished filming, return to your house, pop popcorn, and watch the movie together.

Hot Seats

A minimum of three couples should participate in this activity. To set up, place two chairs back to back in the middle of a room. Seat a couple in these "hot seats" as the first contestants. The other couples find seats around the edges of the room. They are the questioners. To play, the questioners count in unison to three. On the count of three, the contestants each turn their heads either to the right or the left. If they turn their heads in opposite directions, the guy must answer a question from one of the questioners. If they turn their heads in the same direction, the girl must answer the question. One of the questioners asks a question to the appropriate member of the couple such as, "What is your date's favorite flavor of ice cream?" The contestant answers the question and if he is correct, the couple scores a point. If he is incorrect, no point is scored. Play continues until the couple has been asked five questions, after which it trades places with another couple, who takes its turn in the hot seats. The game is over after every couple has had a turn in the hot seats. The couple with the most points at the end of the game wins.

It Happened To Me

For this revealing activity, each participant writes down one of his most embarrassing moments on a piece of paper. Below the experience, he writes his name and the names of two other people in the group, in random order. Someone collects the papers, places them in a hat, and mixes them up. She then selects one paper, reads the experience, and lists the

AFTER-THE-DANCE ACTIVITIES 93

names of the three people on the paper. All three people will claim ownership to the experience. The one to whom the experience really happened must tell the true circumstances around the experience, and the other two people must relate made-up circumstances to try to fool the others. After the three stories have been presented, the rest of the participants vote on who they believe the experience actually happened to. Participants must determine who actually had the experience and which two people are bluffing. When everyone has voted, the real person reveals himself.

Lady Luck And A Chocolate Bar

Buy the biggest chocolate bar you can find for this activity. Set the chocolate bar on a table along with a pair of dice, a fork, and a knife. Also, place on the table some clothing accessories such as a scarf, gloves, glasses, a hat, and a belt. Gather everyone in a circle around the table. The object of this game is for each player to individually eat as much of the chocolate bar as possible. To play, participants take turns rolling the dice onto the table, attempting to roll a lucky number which is either doubles or a seven. When someone gets a lucky number, he immediately puts all of the clothing accessories on as quickly as he can and then eats as much of the chocolate bar as possible. No fingers allowed! The candy bar can only be touched with the fork and knife. As the person dresses and eats, other players continue to roll the dice. As soon as someone else rolls doubles or a seven, she strips the accessories off of the first person, puts them on herself, and eats as much of the chocolate bar as possible. The game continues until the chocolate bar is completely eaten.

Moonlight Volleyball

Go to a park, a beach, or another location at night where you can play volleyball. Divide the couples into two teams and play volleyball by the light of the moon. You may want to use a fluorescent volleyball if you have one, since they tend to be more visible in the dark.

Quarters Maze

This activity requires a group of people, at least two vehicles, and a quarter for each vehicle. Select a starting point and an ending point in your neighborhood. Divide the couples into cars and drive to the starting point. From the starting point, each car begins driving toward the ending point. As the vehicle approaches an intersection, someone in the car flips the quarter. If the quarter comes up heads, the driver must turn left at the intersection. If the quarter comes up tails, the driver must turn right at the intersection. The object of the game is to be the first vehicle to reach the ending point before a designated time period, while obeying all traffic rules. When time has expired, if your car has not reached the ending destination, write down your exact location and then drive to the ending point without following the quarters rule. The first vehicle to reach the ending point before time expires is declared the winner. If none of the vehicles reached the ending point before time expired, the vehicle closest to the ending point when the time expired is the winner.

Service With A Smile

Arrange a service project to perform with your date after the dance. The ideas for possible services are almost limitless, but here are three: get a trash bag and some gloves and pick up trash in a recreational area or along a highway median; obtain some old dolls or stuffed animals and clean them up as well as you can before donating them to charity; wash cars of your and your date's family members as a surprise for them.

Surprise Home Video

For this activity, call your date's parents and ask them to let you borrow some home videos filmed of your date when she was a baby. After the dance, take your date to your house to watch a movie. Watch the surprise on her face as she realizes that she is the main actress in the movie.

Table Sundae

This activity requires a clean table top, a half-gallon cube of ice cream, whipped cream in a can, caramel, fudge, vanilla, nuts, and other sundae toppings. To make your sundae, simply cut the box away from the ice cream. Place the ice cream in the middle of a clean table. Add the toppings to it, making one huge sundae. After blindfolding everyone and seating dates across from each other, give each person a spoon and let him feed his date.

Treasure Hunt

A friend or family member will need to help you with this activity by burying a treasure chest and making a map for you to find it. The trea-

AFTER-THE-DANCE ACTIVITIES 95

sure chest should be filled with snacks, games, and a blanket to sit on. An ice chest or cooler makes a great treasure chest, and a map can be made to look old and somewhat authentic by holding a flame an inch or two below the paper to brown it and singe the edges. Each couple meets at your house, where the map is waiting for you on the table. Follow the clues on the map, taking some small shovels with you. After locating the treasure, dig it out of the dirt, sand, or snow. Open the treasure and enjoy the rest of the evening playing games and snacking on the treats found inside.

Chapter Six

Planning A Dance

Planning a dance can be a great experience. You should have a good committee that includes committee members who are creative, responsible, and willing to work. Depending on how elaborate your dance is going to be, you should plan your first meeting to be held at least a month or two before the event (like a church youth dance), and sometimes up to six or eight months in advance (like prom). At your first committee meeting, there are some basic questions your committee will need to answer:

1. What is your theme?

Selecting a good theme for your dance is critical to successful planning. A theme helps all committee members think along the same lines and use many different ideas to create a whole, finished product. Several ideas for possible dance themes are included in the next chapter of this book.

2. What do you want to have happen at the dance?

This is always a better question than, "What do we want to do at the dance?" The question, "What do we want to have happen" helps you plan with a purpose, so your objectives can be met more effectively. Do you want the people that attend your dance to get acquainted with lots of new friends? Or, do you want to provide a fun event for couples to spend time together? Do you want people to have fun in a casual setting, or would you rather them dress up and have more of a reverent or a ritzy attitude?

PLANNING A DANCE

Asking questions about what you want to have happen at the dance will help your committee focus and gain direction, before you spend time on the more specific planning that will take place next.

3. How much money can you spend?

Before your first meeting, check your budget for the event and be prepared to discuss it with your committee. Make a list of all projected expenses such as invitations, advertising, tickets, decorations, refreshments, music, building rental, etc. Assign committee members to research the probable cost of each expense. If possible, they should find various options for each expense, searching for a price range that includes several different ideas, rather than just one idea and one set price.

For example, the committee member in charge of researching the expense of invitations could consider all of the following options, getting price estimates for each option: printing invitations for every person that may potentially attend the event vs. printing invitations only for people that signify an interest in the event; copying invitations on a copy machine yourselves vs. paying a professional copy store to copy the invitations for you; copying invitations on regular white copy paper vs. copying them onto colored paper, cardstock, or custom paper; and mailing invitations to people's homes vs. hand delivering them.

After you get an idea of how much money you plan to spend, keep within your budget as you allocate money for each expense, and be sure to reserve some money to cover hidden expenses that may arise later. Put at least one responsible committee member in charge of finances, and make sure all expenses are authorized and recorded by this person.

4. Where/when is the dance going to be held?

If you plan to hold your dance in a school gymnasium or a church cultural hall, make sure your event is scheduled with the appropriate activity coordinator and is written on her calendar.

If you plan to hold your dance at a location that requires reservations (a hotel ballroom, a college campus, a government building, a dance hall, etc.), make sure you have contacted the owner or manager of the facility and received permission and reserved scheduling. Many of these types of places charge a fee for letting you use their premises, so make sure you account for that in your budget. Often, hotels will allow you to use one of their ballrooms free of charge if your participants purchase dinner at the hotel as well. This may be an option for you, if you are hosting a dinner/dance. Talk with a hotel coordinator if your are interested in this option.

If you plan to hold your dance at a location that is owned by a person or business (outdoor parking lot, person's home or backyard, etc.), make sure you receive the appropriate person's permission to use his facilities. Also, if your dance will be held outside, let the local police station know of your plans in advance and talk with police officers about limitations on music volume for that area. You may also need to get permission from residents of the area, if your dance will be held near any homes.

In considering a location for your dance, make sure that adequate parking will be available for those who attend. Some locations such as hotel ballrooms may charge a fee to park in their parking lots. If this is the case for you, remember to mention this in your advertising or on the dance tickets. And if you plan to hold your dance outside, always have a backup plan in case of inclement weather.

5. What is the appropriate dress for your dance?

The attire requested for your dance can add tremendously to the atmosphere you create. Appropriate dress can emphasize your theme, promote reverence, add class, or add creativity to your event. Formal, or "black-tie", means tuxedos for the guys, evening gowns for the girls. Semi-formal means suit and tie for the guys, nice dresses or pantsuits for the girls. Casual can mean about anything you specify: nice pants or jeans for both guys and girls, costumes, shorts, or other. Make sure you announce the dress for your dance early in your advertising, to avoid confusion and embarrassment on the day of the event.

6. How do you plan to advertise?

Taking your budget and resources into account, consider any/all of these advertising ideas:
- Posters at school, at church, at grocery stores, at neighboring schools or churches, at community centers.
- Flyers passed out or put on car windshields (make sure this is legal in your area).
- Table top advertisements on school cafeteria tables (table tops are rectangular strips of cardstock about 4" x 11" that you fold length-

PLANNING A DANCE 99

wise into thirds, staple into a triangle, and place on top of tables, that advertise about your dance).
- Sign on the school marquis.
- Sale of tickets at school.
- Announcements at school, church, school assembly, sporting events, or on the radio.
- Advertisements in the local or school newspaper or on church bulletins.
- Invitations passed out or mailed to peoples' homes.

7. What about music?

The two most popular sources of dance music are either a live band or a disc jockey (DJ). There are things to consider when choosing between a live band and a disc jockey. In general, live bands tend to be more expensive than disc jockeys, but provide a unique experience that is unlike listening to the radio. Often, live bands provide entertainment as well as a dance. Disc jockeys often provide a wider range of music to choose from, but they are limited to the music they bring. They often will bring and manage lighting as well as music, which can be helpful. Either of these music sources should be scheduled well in advance (at least a few months), as many of them get booked very quickly. For a list of bands and DJs near you, check with radio stations, in the phone book, or with local teenagers who often can give you referrals.

If neither a live band nor a DJ fits into your plans or your budget, other music options are available. For instance, if you plan to hold your dance in a parking lot, you could have all the participants that drive to the dance park their cars in a huge circle facing inward, leave their cars running, turn on their headlights, and tune their radios to the same station. Turn up the radios and dance to the radio music inside the circle of cars. Another example is to ask everyone who attends the dance to bring his favorite music (labeled with his name on it) for a volunteer DJ to use throughout the event with a sound system brought from home. Make sure a responsible person watches the music throughout the dance and returns it to its proper owners when the dance is over.

8. What about decorations?

Although decorations are not necessary for a fun dance (and sometimes are not even possible based on its location), they can add a great deal to the atmosphere and can accentuate your theme well. Plan decorations around your theme for a more complete effect.

Decorations come in all types. Your committee can make them itself using crepe paper, scissors, and glue, you can borrow them or rent them from a local rental store, or you can purchase them. If decorations are purchased and if you act in behalf of an organization that puts on dances on a regular basis, consider storing them with the organization for future use. They can come in very handy at a later date!

9. And what about refreshments?

Because dancing makes almost everyone hot and sweaty (yes, even the girls!), it is a good idea to provide at least drinks at your dance. Cold water, punch, or juice work well. Soda pop is also popular, but remember that soda pop does not quench thirst as well as some other beverages. Drinks served out of a punch bowl allow for refills without wasting excess cups. Relying on a drinking fountain to provide participants with drinks can be disastrous at a dance if a lot of people are thirsty all at once (like just after a good song ends). Serving drinks, even if it's just water, is worth the effort.

If you want to offer a food item, stick with something light like cookies or fruit to avoid giving people side aches. Finger foods are easy for people to handle and are quick at getting people back out onto the dance floor. Provide small plates or napkins for serving food items, even if it's just finger foods you're offering. Also, provide several garbage cans at various locations, so the area doesn't get cluttered with used paper products.

You can set up one refreshment table for people to file by, or you can add tables for people to sit at and relax while they enjoy the refreshments you've provided. However, keep in mind that as a general rule, more tables equals less dancing. Providing tables and chairs encourages people to sit instead of dance, and may contradict the purpose of your event.

You will want to have a few people attending the refreshment table during the dance to fill cups, to refill platters, and to clean up messes. Maybe parents, teachers, youth leaders, or younger brothers or sisters of people attending the dance would be willing to help with this.

10. How about pictures?

For most school dances for couples, a photographer and his crew are on site during the dance to take pictures of interested couples, to be developed and returned to the couples at a later date. This is an opportunity for you to make a little money for your school, as sometimes photographers provide a kickback of a dollar or two per set of pictures ordered, to contribute to the school.

Select a photographer and reserve a room for him to use throughout the event. The room should provide adequate lighting for the photographer, and should be big enough to accommodate a long line of couples. It should be close enough to the dance to be accessible, but far enough away that it doesn't distract from the dance.

After you have answered these questions, you will have a pretty good outline of your event. Now, it's time to make assignments. Give each committee member something to do, and hold follow up meetings to make sure everyone follows through with his/her assignments.

Following is a sample checklist that you might use on the day of the event to make sure your bases are covered:

- Building is unlocked before committee arrives.
- Decorations gathered and at location.
- Decoration committee arrives at proper set up time.
- Food and service (napkins, cups, plates etc.) arrive, with ample storage and refrigeration for it.
- Music person/people arrive to set up at least 1-2 hours before the dance.
- Photographer and crew arrive at least 1-2 hours before the dance.
- Food servers arrive at least 30 minutes before the dance.
- Ticket takers arrive at least 30 minutes before the dance.
- All receipts turned in for purchases made.

Chapter Seven

Ideas for Dance Themes

Animal Dance
Decorate with pictures of different kinds of animals. Your setting could have animals living in their natural habitats, in cages at the zoo, or on a circus train. Serve animal crackers for refreshments.

Armed Forces Dance
Everyone dresses like a member of the armed forces. Serve Meals Ready To Eat (MREs) for refreshments. MREs can be purchased at an emergency supply store or an army/navy store. Decorate with army paraphernalia such as camouflage nets, parachutes, and army tents. Refreshments could be served inside an erected army tent. Visiting a military surplus store would provide more decorative ideas.

Babes In Toyland Dance
Everyone must donate a small, new toy for admittance to this dance. Decorate with large stuffed animals and other toys. You might even construct a huge cardboard toy factory. Decorate the refreshment area with a toy kitchen set, and place its accompanying plastic food and dishes on the refreshment table as well. Participants could come dressed up as action figures, dolls, or toys. After the dance, donate the new toys people have brought to a charitable organization to be distributed to needy children.

Baby Photo Dance
Participants bring baby photos of themselves and come looking as much like their baby photos as possible. Judge the participants as they enter the dance, and award the winners during the dance. Carefully and creatively

IDEAS FOR DANCE THEMES

display the baby photos near the refreshment area. Give each photo a number, and let participants try to guess who's who as they look at the display. On the back of the display, provide a ledger which has each person's name by the number of his photo.

Back To School Dance

This dance is held in honor of the beginning of another school year, and should be planned for all incoming students, not just for couples. Decorate with school paraphernalia such as paper, pencils, textbooks, apples, and report cards. Use your school colors and mascot for decorations, unless students from more than one school are invited to attend. Serve refreshments on cafeteria trays.

Backwards Dance

Everyone wears his/her clothes backwards to this dance. In the parking lot, set up a sign which welcomes participants to the Backwards Dance and requests them to pull into their parking stalls in reverse and walk up to the building backwards. Keep the front door to the building closed, of course. Use the back door as the main entry. Serve upside-down cake for refreshments. On a couple of slow songs, instruct everyone to try to dance back to back. (Playing the music backwards is not recommended!)

Beach Dance

Have this dance at the beach, or decorate your dance hall to look like a beach. Decorations could include beach balls, a volleyball net, surfing boards, lawn chairs, fish, bubbles, mermaids, and seashells. All servers and ticket takers should wear sunglasses and floral prints. Serve fruit or fish-shaped cookies for refreshments.

Bermuda Triangle Dance

Everyone wears Bermuda shorts and/or patterns with triangles on them. Decorate with triangles. Serve triangular shaped foods for refreshments such as pizza, fruit pizza, pie, or triangle-shaped cookies (bake big, round cookies and slice them like a pizza into triangular slices).

"Candy Land" Dance

Adorn the walls of your dance hall with huge paper or cardboard lollipops, gingerbread houses, candy canes, gingerbread men, gumdrops, cinnamon bears, and other candies. You might use Hansel and Gretel in your decor as well. For refreshments, of course, serve candy!

Celebrity Look-Alike Dance

Everyone dresses up to look like a celebrity, and tries to guess who each other resembles throughout the dance. Awards could be given to the best look-alikes. Decorate your dance hall to look like Hollywood. Make the refreshments area look like a movie studio with a director's chair, spotlights on the food, a megaphone, etc.

Christmas Dance

Decorate the dance hall to look like Santa's workshop or like a winter wonderland. Fake snow can be purchased and scattered around the floor, for a wintry effect. Snowmen and snowflakes could adorn the walls, and snow cones could be served for refreshments. A good theme for a Christmas dance would be the "Jingle Bell Rock."

City Nights

Decorate your dance hall to resemble a big city at night. You could make silhouettes of buildings out of cardboard, spray paint them black, and stand them in front of a wall. Plug lights in behind them that point upwards, giving the effect of a lighted city behind the buildings.

Color Wheel Dance

Upon entering, each participant is given a red, yellow, blue, or white card. As a song begins, a color caller holds up a large colored card that is a color made by mixing two of the four basic colors together. For example, if he holds up a green card, then blues and yellows dance with each other; if he holds up a pink card, then reds and whites dance with each other. Whenever he holds up a black card, however, participants can dance with whomever they choose. After each song, participants can trade cards with someone else.

Country/Western Dance

For this dance, one of the best investments you will make is that of a good caller. Hire someone that is good with a microphone and can call for square dancing, line dancing, and other country dances. You could decorate with bales of hay, saddles, and pictures of cowboys. Have everyone dress in western clothing, and serve apple pie or apple cider for refreshments.

IDEAS FOR DANCE THEMES

Cowboys And Indians

For this dance, you could have couples decide whether to dress up as a cowboy couple or an Indian couple, or you could have guys be cowboys and girls be Indians, or vice versa. Decorate your dance hall to look like the Wild West, with horses, buffalo, saddles, cactus plants, lassos, tepees, and mountains. Your theme might be, "The Wild Wild West."

Dance Cards

Dance cards are small cards with several numbered blank lines, which the owner must have signed by each person he dances with during the evening. They encourage participants to dance with lots of different people throughout the event. Pass out dance cards to all the participants as they enter the dance hall. A prize could be offered to the first person to turn in a completed dance card during the evening. Make sure every line is signed by a different person!

Dancing In The Rain

To decorate for this dance, hang silver streamers or tinsel from white paper clouds to resemble rain. Make a large rainbow, raindrops, gray clouds, and lightning bolts to adorn the walls. Participants could dress up with raincoats, umbrellas, and galoshes. Since rain brings worms out of the ground, you could purchase "Gummy Worms" from a candy store to serve for refreshments.

"Dear" Hunt Dance

This dance is especially effective in the Fall during deer hunting season. Participants wear fluorescent orange (hunter orange). Decorate with a fake campfire, back packs, sleeping bags, tents, a forest, and deer. Refreshments could be "S'mores" (little sandwiches made by putting a roasted marshmallow and a few squares of a chocolate bar in between two graham crackers) or "deer pellets" (chocolate covered raisins). If you host this dance for couples, advertise that participants should come with their "dears"; if not, have them come to the dance to find a "dear."

Destiny Dance

Make two sets of numbers on small cards before the dance, one set of blue cards and one set of pink cards. Give a blue number to each guy and a pink number to each girl as everyone arrives. Participants have to find their same-numbered people during the evening. A prize could be given to the first couple to find each other.

Dinosaur Dance

Decorate with pictures of dinosaurs, dinosaur eggs, and prehistoric vegetation. Serve deviled eggs, "Gummy Dinosaurs" gummy candies, or dinosaur-shaped cookies for refreshments.

Disco Dance

Dress for the 1970's for this dance. Make sure to have a bunch of groovy music on hand, as well as someone to teach everyone how to disco. For a really authentic touch, play your music with either an eight-track player or a record player. Display posters or record covers of famous music groups from the 1970's. Attach bell bottom pants, silk shirts, and other clothing from the 1970's to the walls.

Disney Dance

Everyone dresses up like his favorite Walt Disney character or like a member of the Mickey Mouse Club. During the evening, announce dances specifically for certain Disney movies in which characters from that movie dance with each other. Decorate with Disney paraphernalia, such as title banners of Disney animated movies and scenes from Disneyland or Disney World, such as the Matterhorn. Mickey Mouse shaped cookies could be served for refreshments.

Dummy Dance

Give a guy a girl dummy and a girl a guy dummy. The guy and girl dance with their dummies for at least 30 seconds before handing off their dummies to two people who are not dancing and selecting real people to dance with. The new dummy-holders must dance with their dummies for at least 30 seconds before passing them to two new people and replacing them with real people.

Falling Leaves Dance

For a dance to be held in the Fall, decorate with rakes and red, orange, yellow, and brown leaves (real or made from construction paper). Make a large paper tree for one wall which has bare branches. Have each participant put his or her name on a leaf and tape it face down on a branch of the tree. Girls should put their leaves on one side of the tree and the guys on the other. Every so often, announce a guy's or girl's choice leaf dance in which each participant comes to the tree, grabs a leaf, turns it over to find the name of the person on his leaf, and dances with the person whose name is on his leaf.

IDEAS FOR DANCE THEMES

Fiesta Dance

Decorate Mexican style, including a large sun, cactus plants, sombreros, and pinatas filled with candy. Hold a pinata breaking contest during the dance. Serve tortilla chips and bean dip for refreshments. You might even teach the dance "La Cucaracha" to participants during the event.

Fifties Dance

For this dance, participants dress up like they were part of the 1950's era. Provide music from the 1950's to dance to. Decorate with records and pictures of old cars. For refreshments, serve sodas with straws.

Fruit And Vegetables Dance

Each person must bring a can of fruit or vegetables for admittance to the dance. Decorate with fruit baskets and serve fresh fruit and vegetables or fruit cocktail for refreshments. After the dance, donate the canned food to the needy.

Galaxy Dance

Decorations could include the nine planets, astronauts, rocket ships, stars, meteorites, even aliens and UFO's from outer space. For drinks, you might serve "Sunny Delight" citrus drink or "Sunkist" soda pop. For refreshments, serve "Starbursts" wrapped fruit candies or chocolate bars like "Mars" or "Milky Way."

Graduation Dance

This dance honors graduates, so it should not be planned for couples. Everyone who is graduating should have the opportunity to attend and enjoy the event. Music for the dance should consist of music of the era of the participants at the time of their graduation. Entertainment during this dance could include humorous awards to graduates, a slide show, or other ideas that help participants remember their experiences before graduating.

Hair Dance

For this dance, participants wear the wildest hairdos they can create on themselves. Awards could be given during the event to recognize the funniest, weirdest, scariest, prettiest, or classiest hairdos. Serve Chocolate "Mousse" for dessert.

Halloween Dance

For this dance, everyone wears his Halloween costume. Decorate the dance hall as either a haunted house or a cemetery with witches, ghosts, and other ghouls. Jack-o-lanterns could decorate the refreshment table. You might serve tombstone-shaped pumpkin cookies for refreshments. If you use a haunted house theme, serve peeled grapes in a bowl labeled "eyeballs" and spaghetti noodles labeled "brains."

Hat Dance

Participants must wear a hat for admission to this dance. During the dance, you could give awards for the most creative hats worn. Also, you might host a hat exchange during the dance, in which everyone exchanges hats with whomever he dances with. During the dance, participants will see their hats on several different people's heads. Be sure they get their own hats back before they go home!

Hawaiian Luau

Decorate your dance hall as if you were in Hawaii. Remember the palm trees, pineapples, beaches, and flowers. People could wear grass skirts over their flower-print clothes. Pass out leis at the door as participants enter. For refreshments, serve a fruit platter or fruit drinks with little umbrellas.

Headphones Dance

Each person brings a walkman with her own music, and everyone dances on the dance floor together, listening to different kinds of music. Give your dance mate an ear bud for a slow dance. There shouldn't be any complaints about the type of music played during the event, and participants can be slow dancing and fast dancing all at once! Another bonus: if your dance is held outside, the neighbors won't mind the volume.

Heaven And Hell Dance

The guys come dressed in red and the girls come dressed in white, or vice versa. Decorate with angels and devils, flames and clouds, halos and pitchforks. Serve angel food cake and devil's food cake for refreshments, or white jelly beans and "Red Hots" or "Hot Tamales" candies.

International Dance

Decorate your dance hall like a foreign country or have areas reserved to look like several different foreign countries which partici-

IDEAS FOR DANCE THEMES

pants can visit throughout the dance. Everyone dresses up like a citizen of one of the featured countries. Refreshments should be authentic foods or drinks from the selected countries. Another way to host this dance would be to allow participants to dress in clothes from any foreign country they desire. Refreshments would be a variety of different foods from foreign countries.

Jelly Bean Dance

Put equal numbers of colored jelly beans in one dish for guys and one for girls. Pass out one jelly bean to each participant upon entering the dance. Each person must find a guy or girl to dance with that has the same color of jelly bean as he has. After the song is over, participants can eat their jelly beans and choose new ones, as long as they always find people to dance with that have the same color of jelly beans as they do.

Jungle Dance

Decorate your dance hall to look like a jungle with vines, monkeys, tigers, and even Tarzan and Jane. Serve wild animal crackers, bananas, red licorice vines, or tropical drinks for refreshments. You could have a "Tarzan Call" contest or a "Chimpanzee Call" contest to get things "swinging."

Masquerade Dance

Before holding this dance, make sure that masks are allowed at the premises you have reserved for the dance. Everyone comes to the dance wearing the mask of his choice, and all masks must be worn throughout the dance. The song "Masquerade" from the Broadway show *Phantom of The Opera* could be used as a theme song for this event.

Media Dance

Center the theme of this dance around a popular movie, TV show, or song on the radio. You could ask participants to dress like characters from the movie or TV show you have chosen.

Morp

Morp is "prom" spelled backwards, and that's just what this dance is: a backwards prom night! Girls do the asking and the paying, and the dress is casual (can be costume-oriented).

Mystery Dance

Upon entering, everyone is tagged with a name of a famous person on his back. During the dance, participants can ask each person they dance with two or three questions that can be answered with only a "Yes" or "No" answer, in an attempt to figure out who they are. The person who finds out who he is after the least amount of dances wins a prize.

New Year's Eve Dance

For this dance, start late enough that you can end after midnight and keep people having fun the whole time. Provide party hats, blow horns, balloons, confetti, and a large TV so participants can celebrate as they watch the countdown to the new year. After the stroke of midnight, you could serve a New Year's Day breakfast before the dance is over.

Noah's Ark Dance

Couples come as pairs of animals. Decorate with an ark, rain, a dove, and a rainbow. Serve animal crackers for refreshments.

Number Dance

As people arrive for this dance, give them each a card with a number between 1 and 7 written on it. As a song begins, everyone hunts for a person of his same number with whom to dance. After each song, the guys trade their numbers with other guys and the girls trade their numbers with other girls, and the search for new partners begins again as a new song begins. You can adjust the range of numbers to be 1-5 or 1-10, based on the number of people who attend the dance.

Pajama Party Dance

Everyone comes in her pajamas to this dance. No shoes allowed: only slippers. Decorate with blankets, pillows, teddy bears, and bedtime story books. Serve cookies and milk for refreshments.

Picture Perfect Dance

In preparation for this dance, look through several magazines and pull out pages which have just one person dominating the page. Then, cut the picture in half vertically, straight down the middle of the page. Separate the halves into two piles, one for the guys and one for the girls. As participants enter the dance, give each of them a picture of a half of a person. During the dance, they find partners with whom to dance and

IDEAS FOR DANCE THEMES

at the end of each song, they show their partners their half person pictures, hoping their halves match up with their partners' halves to make complete pictures of whole people. Give an award to the couple that first completes its picture correctly.

Pioneer Dance

Decorate with pictures of covered wagons, teams of oxen, horses, or mules, and log cabins. Also, place a fake campfire in the middle of the dance floor. Everyone dresses like a pioneer, with girls in bonnets and aprons and guys in cowboy hats and suspenders. For refreshments, serve hardtack. (Hardtack, a staple that was often eaten by pioneers on the trail, can be made by mixing flour and water into a dough, rolling it out about 1/4 inch thick, and then baking it for a long time in a slow oven. When it is completely hard, break it into bite-size pieces and serve.)

President's Ball

Each couple comes dressed as a famous president and his wife. Decorate with pictures of past presidents. Throughout the dance, between songs, provide bits of presidential trivia or hold a contest like "Name That President."

Pumpkin Patch Dance

For this Fall dance, hold a contest to see who can bring the biggest, smallest, or best looking pumpkin. Use the pumpkins as decorations. During the event, you could have a pumpkin carving contest as well. Serve pumpkin pie or pumpkin cookies for refreshments.

Radio Road Dance

This dance should be held in an outdoor parking lot or other paved area after receiving permission by the owner of the lot. Ask the people that drive to this dance to park their cars in a big circle with all of their headlights facing inward. The circle inside the cars will provide a well-lit dance floor. You might even cover some of the headlights with colored plastic wrap to create colored lighting. Instruct each driver to tune his radio to the same radio station and turn up the volume. Dance to the music on your improvised dance floor. You might want to call the radio station in advance and inform it of your dance, to see if it will play your requests throughout the evening.

Rainbow Dance

Decorate with rainbows and balloons that are the seven colors of the rainbow: red, orange, yellow, green, blue, indigo, and violet. Everyone dresses in rainbow colors. Serve rainbow "Jello" for refreshments. (To make rainbow "Jello", purchase small boxes of "Jello" in as many colors as you wish. Make up one box of "Jello" by following the directions on the box and then pour a thin layer of it into a large, clear casserole dish and let it set until firm. Make up a second box of "Jello" in a different color and pour a thin layer of it on top of first layer, letting it set until firm. Continue layering "Jello" as desired.)

Rock-N-Roll Dance

Advertise this dance well in advance so that participants can make arrangements to obtain roller blades for use at the dance. Participants come wearing roller blades and literally "rock and roll" to the music. Be sure the dance floor surface is suitable for the roller blades, and obtain permission beforehand to use roller blades there.

Sailor Dance

For this dance, participants dress like sailors. You might decorate with sailboats, ropes, anchors, fish, and Popeye. You could serve spinach dip and crackers or salt water taffy for refreshments.

Saint Patrick's Day Dance

Everyone wears all green for this dance, which should be held on or near March 17. Decorate with shamrocks and leprechauns. Put green food coloring in the cookies or other refreshments, and serve green punch to drink. Cups, napkins, and other decor should also be green.

Sizzlin' Summer Dance

This dance is held outside as the heat of the summer day fades into a warm summer night. Shorts, T-shirts, and sandals are allowed. Serve "Kool-Aid" or lemonade to drink.

Sock Hop

No shoes allowed at this definitely indoor dance. Everyone leaves his shoes at the door and dances in his socks. Decorate by hanging all sorts

IDEAS FOR DANCE THEMES

of socks of different shapes, sizes, and colors on the walls and from the ceiling. Teach the "Sock Hop" to all participants.

Somewhere In Time Dance

For this dance, everyone dresses up in a costume of any time period in history. Decorate with clocks, calendars, watches, hourglasses, sun dials, and maybe even a time-travel machine. Be sure to play the theme song from the movie *Somewhere In Time* for a slow dance.

Super Hero Dance

Everyone comes to this dance dressed up as a favorite super hero. You might let participants dance to the theme songs of *Superman, Batman, Spiderman,* and *Wonder Woman* during the event. You could serve "kryptonite" (green "Jello" or green "Rice Krispie" treats) for refreshments.

Take A Chance Dance

Each participant brings five personal articles which are so unique that they are distinctively his. (The more inexpensive and less attached participants are to them, the better, just in case they are not all returned.) The girls enter on one side of the dance hall and place their items on tables, and the guys do the same at the other end of the dance hall. When dance music begins, each guy selects an object and mingles among the girls, searching for the owner of the object he selected. When he finds the owner, he dances with her. For the next song, each girl approaches the guys' table, chooses an object, and finds her partner. (After each object has been used, place it under the table so that each object is used only once.)

Toga Dance

Decorate your dance hall to look like ancient Italy or Greece. Include tall, white marble pillars, marble statues, and greenery. Hang Greek letters or words such as Sigma, Alpha, Gamma, and Beta from the ceilings or on the walls and hold a contest to see who can properly identify each Greek letter of the alphabet. Participants could wear togas and green-leaf halos. Serve grapes for refreshments.

Treasure Island Dance

Participants dress like pirates or castaways. Decorate with pirate ships, Jolly Rogers, treasure chests filled with gold coins and jewels, plastic swords, and deserted islands. For entertainment during this dance, you could hide a treasure or pass out hints to find a treasure based on the number of people one dances with. Refreshments could include gold foil covered chocolate coins and punch called "Grog."

Ugly Tie Dance

For this dance, guys and girls must wear the ugliest ties they can find. During the dance, have an ugly tie contest, letting the girls judge the guys and the guys judge the girls.

Uncle Sam Jam

Decorate with American flags, fireworks on the walls, and pictures of Presidents of the United States. Participants must wear only red, white, and blue. On one wall, list several historical facts about the administrations of the different Presidents, all in scrambled order. During the event, participants can try to match the facts to the proper Presidents, write their answers on index cards, and drop them into a box. At the end of the dance, give an award to whomever unscrambled the most facts correctly.

Under The Sea Dance

Decorate the dance hall with fish, seashells, ocean waves, anchors, sunken ships, submarines, mermaids, and seaweed. Serve saltwater taffy or fish crackers for refreshments.

Up And Down Dance

Before the dance, make a list of about ten familiar sayings that include 'and' in them such as "Up and Down," "Macaroni and Cheese," "Right and Left," "Potatoes and Gravy," "Bread and Butter," and "Silver and Gold." Get a stack of index cards (estimate one card for every two people you plan to have in attendance at your dance) and write one of the ten sayings on each card. Cut the cards in half vertically, straight through the word 'and,' putting one half in a pile for the guys and one half in a pile for the girls. At the dance, hand out the cards to the guys and girls. Everyone finds a person whose card completes her saying properly and dances with him. After the dance, everyone can trade cards with someone of the same sex and do it again.

Valentine's Day Dance

For this holiday dance, decorate with red, white, and pink hearts and Cupid with his bows and arrows. Serve Valentine chocolates or heart-

IDEAS FOR DANCE THEMES 115

shaped cookies and red or pink punch for refreshments. Decorate the refreshment table with red roses and candy hearts.

Video Dance

About a month before this dance, assign a video crew to videotape people that plan on attending this upcoming dance. The crew should video segments of people in a variety of settings such as at home, at school, at sporting events, at work, in their cars, or on a date. Set the video to dance music. On the day of the event, set up several TV/VCRs and play the videos while you dance to the music on the tape.